W9-AOS-382

enchanted adornments

Creating MIXED~MEDIA Jewelry *with* Metal Clay, Wire, Resin + More

cynthia thornton

INTERWEAVE
interweavestore.com

To all the wonderful folks who have, throughout the years, shown me support and provided me with honesty, friendship, and the knowledge that they'd be at my side the moment I needed them . . . or at least be on the phone.

PROJECT PHOTOGRAPHY Annette Slade and Brad Bartholomew
STEP PHOTOGRAPHY Joe Coca
COVER + INTERIOR DESIGN Pamela Norman
PHOTO STYLING Pam Chavez
ILLUSTRATIONS + PAINTINGS Cynthia Thornton
PRODUCTION Katherine Jackson
EDITOR Darlene D'Agostino
TECHNICAL EDITORS Andrew Thornton and Danielle Fox

Interweave Press LLC
201 East 4th Street
Loveland, CO 80537-5655 USA
interweavestore.com

Printed in China by Asia Pacific Offset Ltd.

Library of Congress Cataloging-in-Publication Data

Thornton, Cynthia, 1974-
  Enchanted adornments : creating mixed-media jewelry
with metal clay, wire, resin, and more /
Cynthia Thornton.
     p. cm.
  Includes index.
  ISBN 978-1-59668-157-6 (pbk.)
  1. Jewelry making. I. Title.
  TT212.T563 2009
  739.27--dc22

                    2009023431

10 9 8 7 6 5 4 3 2 1

acknowledgments

A book is one of those things that starts as an inkling and grows according to how much nurturing that idea receives. This particular project has had the benefit of my family and friends to provide much-needed encouragement along the way.

Over the years I've known lots of metal workers who have gone out of their way to make sure I was doing things right. Two of them became friends and mentors whom I admire and deeply respect: Anne Choi, for always steering me straight and encouraging me to go just a little bit farther than I thought I could go, and Bob Burkett, for teaching me wax work, even though I was sure I'd never get it. Thank you both for never giving up on me.

Without my family, this book would still be an idea. I couldn't have managed without my husband, Greg, my hero, who saved countless days with his cookie-baking skills. My daughter, Azalea, who helped me condition loads of polymer. The biggest thank-you of all goes to my brother Andrew, because without him, I'd probably still be working on this book. Thanks, Brother, for being a taskmaster, wire wrapper, and resin-pouring mad scientist!

contents

introduction

As a child, I knew that objects, especially ones made by hand, held magic. I once owned an amulet, a little silver bird in flight strung on a fine chain. The originator, an elderly Native American man, assured me of its power to grant the wearer fleetness of foot, and I believed him. Wearing it, I could run faster than my brother or sister, and I could beat every kid on the block in a race, tearing past cacti and tumbleweeds.

Growing up under the shade of folktales and superstitions, my view of the world has always been tinted with magic. Tales from my mother's father, who was a medicine man of the Pacific Islands, drifted down and blanketed us grandchildren in a fine web of stories. Sea monsters can swallow you whole. Mermaids do indeed drag foolish folks under. Pearls protect a swimmer from sharks. These odd remnants from forgotten times settled deep within my soul, and this idea that objects can hold wishes, blessings, or hope will continue to be passed on to my own children.

I have always made things. As a child, everything was a viable material, from collected bits from the road and broken pieces of jewelry to seashells and pretty rocks. The love of creating continues to follow me, and although I now use different materials, the desire to make objects that hold a little magic has never waned. I have collected my favorite materials and formulas to share, hoping and wishing with all my heart that they inspire others in the world.

HOW TO USE THIS BOOK

Creating your own magical objects is easy. This book, divided into four parts, will show you how. It uniquely combines my love of storytelling with a wide variety of innovative jewelry techniques meant to teach unexpected ways to create one-of-a-kind pieces infused with personal meaning. Presented like an artist's sketchbook, it is full of my own drawings, paintings, an original short story, and photographs to inspire and guide you on your journey.

There are a couple of ways to utilize the information within these pages. The first is to find a project you like and dig in, referring back to the first two chapters for tips to complete the piece. The second, and most useful, is to start from the beginning, read through the Basics and Essentials chapters and then dive into the projects chapter. Once there, read the diary entry that precedes the project so that you can understand the inspiration for the design of the jewelry. This part of the book is designed to illustrate the conceptual aspects of the Inspiration chapter, mainly dissecting an idea and turning it into a piece of art. Through the entries and then sketches, one can see how a kernel of inspiration is transformed into jewelry, with echoes of the original idea. The entries also illuminate the process of designing for an individual and deciphering vague clues to create a piece that suits them perfectly.

the basics

FINDING & HARNESSING INSPIRATION

Magic cannot be created without inspiration. There needs to be a spark to ignite the process and intention of creating objects that hypnotize and captivate. Objects that aren't inspired are dull and generic. They won't evoke the interest of others, nor will they help bring magic into your everyday life. Some people are blessed with the innate ability to recognize and harness inspiration. Others have to create a practice out of it. The pages that follow will give you the necessary tools and methods so that you can summon inspiration and use it to propel your imagination into the act of creation.

inspiration

Every creative endeavor requires some type of inspiration to fuel the process, and it can arrive in any form—a person, music, nature, a favorite place—pretty much anything can ignite an idea. The road between an idea and a finished piece is a winding one that starts and stops, changes directions, and may not resemble the original thought in the end.

the sketchbook

The sketchbook is the all-important tool for capturing fleeting inspiration. It is quite versatile: You can store ideas, phone numbers, bits of overheard conversation, little maps to favorite places, and you can tape in flowers and ephemera. Soon your sketchbook is not only a palette of ideas but also documentation of your existence. Carry it everywhere, along with some type of colorant, such as a set of colored pencils or mini watercolor paints, which will be useful for capturing interesting palette combinations. A fine-tip Sakura Micron pen will last a long time, and it won't bleed or change color. A roll of clear matte tape is a fun addition, good for adhering small things to pages and sealing flowers to preserve their color and form.

*note DON'T EVER TEAR OUT PAGES FROM YOUR SKETCHBOOK. THOSE YOU PERCEIVE AS "BAD" WILL SHOW PROGRESSION + YOU CAN ALWAYS EITHER GESSO OVER THEM OR ADHERE A PHOTO OR OTHER ITEM ON TOP.

*note GET INTO THE HABIT OF STUDYING YOUR SURROUNDINGS. THIS DOESN'T MEAN STOPPING + GAPING AT EVERY LEAF, BUT TRYING TO PICK OUT INTERESTING COLORS, BEAUTIFUL SHAPES + INTRIGUING PATTERNS AS YOU GO BY.

drawing

Drawing is a wonderful activity for encouraging creativity.

~During the design phase, it is essential for idea conceptualization.

~It can be meditative, freeing your mind of stress and opening it to inspiration.

~If just beginning to draw, deconstruct objects into outlines, large shapes, and basic forms.

~Once satisfied with your drawing of basic shapes, begin working on the details.

look books & inspiration boards

Look books and inspiration boards are the perfect places to collect inspired ideas.

~**CAPTURE** colors or images that move you inside a blank book or on a board.

~**INCLUDE** sketches, color palettes, and images.

~**SEARCH** the Internet, catalogs, magazines, fabrics, etc., for images and ideas.

~**SEE** a story emerge in the form of color, pattern, line quality, and mood.

~**CREATE + ORGANIZE** by category— nature, jewelry, architecture, etc.

*****note** CREATE AN INSPIRATION PACK. PROCURE OR MAKE A NIFTY SATCHEL + FILL IT WITH A SKETCHBOOK, FAVORITE PEN, ARTIST TAPE, COLORED PENCILS + WHATEVER OTHER CREATIVE ACCOUTREMENTS YOU'D LIKE ON HAND WHEN INSPIRATION STRIKES. KEEP IT WITH YOU ALWAYS.

deconstruction

A simple method to harness inspiration into usable fuel is deconstruction: Break down the individual elements that comprise the whole and examine them. The resulting piece will materialize from the elements you choose. Let's use the ocean as the inspiration for a necklace and break it down into its basic parts, which are color, texture, and shape.

{
COLOR The pale green of sea foam, darkest teal of deep water, orangey red of coral, and tawny beige of sand

TEXTURE Fluid, grainy, pebbled, wavy

SHAPE Long strips for the shore line, curves for waves, circles for bubbly froth
}

An object can be deconstructed on a very basic level, such as the example above, or you can intensely deconstruct until the results are only a murmur of the whole.

Use the same method to analyze inspiration that isn't visual, such as a song or personal experience. The results will be much more unique because you are pulling from your individual memories and moods. The basic elements of a song might be mood (how it makes you feel), memories (what you think of when you hear it), and time period (present, past, or future, and what season it evokes).

When designing for an individual, deconstruction is very useful. Think of the colors that this person wears; in what type of setting will the piece be worn (casual, formal); what shape would flatter his or her body and personality. The more information you can deduce will make it more likely that you will capture the essence of this person and therefore what this person would like.

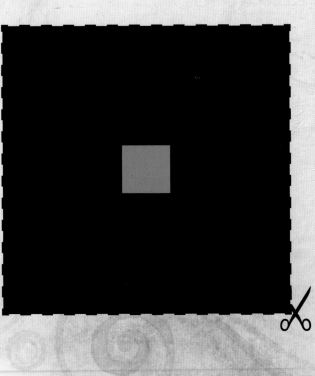

*__note__ TO REVIEW COLOR SELECTION, ISOLATE INDIVIDUAL COLORS FROM THE REST IN THE PROJECT. CREATE A VIEWFINDER FROM A SCRAP OF BLACK OR GRAY CARD STOCK BY CUTTING A ½" (1.3 CM) SQUARE IN THE CENTER. CENTER THE COLOR TO BE REVIEWED IN THE HOLE + YOU WILL SEE IT WITHOUT THE SURROUNDING COLORS CLOUDING ITS TRUE SHADE.

symbolism

Symbolism is a language that transcends words and sounds. It transmits its meaning through images. Symbols can convey any emotion or meaning, and as artists, it is wise to understand the symbols used in our work. Symbols can change meaning over time, but some are eternal, such as that of a tree, always standing for strength, shelter, and growth. The image of a bird is freedom and a lion, power. There are hundreds of meanings for objects. Study what you are drawn to or consistently create—what do they say? Choose your symbols wisely because they represent you. Dive deep into who you are and what you love. Follow this thread, and it will weave its way into your work and gradually infuse it with layers of meaning. This will take time, but your work will strike a chord and resonate.

A LIST OF UNIVERSAL SYMBOLS

ACORN
potential, life

APPLE
love, temptation, Eve

BEES
productivity

BIRDS
freedom, the soul

BOTTLE
womb, enclosure

BUTTERFLY
immortality, metamorphosis

CAT
stealth, liberty

CIRCLE
totality, eternity

CROW
bad luck, death

DEER
speed, gentleness

DOG
loyalty

DOOR
opportunity, passage

DRAGONFLY
summer, speed

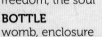

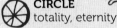

EGG
universe, creation

EYE
protection

FEATHER
truth

FLOWERS
the feminine, growth

GOLD
the sun

HAND
tool, friends, protection

HEART
center of being, love, life blood

HORNS
power of the soul

HORSE
noble, power of the sea

KEY
opening, closing, knowledge

LEAF
renewal, growth

LINES
division, boundaries

MASK
concealment, transformation

MERMAID
the sea, duality

OCTOPUS
cleverness, spirals

OWL
wisdom, night

PEARL
power of water

RABBIT
trickster

ROCK
permanence

SNAIL
birth, eternity, labyrinth

SNAKE
resurrection, underworld

SKULL
mortality, transition

SPIRAL
continuity, water

STAR
constancy, hope

TURTLE
time, longevity

WINGS
transcendence, the supernatural

✱**note** AVOID USING IMAGERY BECAUSE IT IS POPULAR + YOU WANT IT TO MAKE YOUR ART MARKETABLE. LOOK FURTHER TO FIND IMAGES THAT ARE POWERFUL TO YOU.

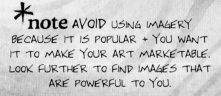

the essentials

UNDERSTANDING THE PROPERTIES
OF WIRE, POLYMER CLAY, PRECIOUS
METAL CLAY, RESIN + MORE

To imbue jewelry with magic, all that is necessary is an understanding of a few key materials. Here, you will learn the basic principles for working with wire, polymer clay, Precious Metal Clay, and resin as well as a brief tutorial on mold making.

Make sure you are working in a well-ventilated area with windows—have fans and a dust mask around, too. Good task lighting will help prevent eyestrain, and long, deep work tables will ensure you have plenty of room (by the way, aluminum rimmed cookie sheets are excellent for storing unfinished projects). You'll want to find a comfortable chair that supports your lumbar area—armrests will ease shoulder stress.

Organize your tools so that they are within easy reach and have rubber mats and ceramic tiles on hand for cutting and working with heat, respectively. When working with a torch, be mindful to keep the torch away from curtains and anything else flammable. When you are engrossed in your work, it's hard to be cognizant of such potential disasters; therefore, a fire extinguisher is a necessity! Finally, create ambience so that your space invites your creativity. Keep inspiration everywhere you can see.

wire

USE WIRE for creating chains, earrings, wrapping stones without holes, making bails, and as a beautiful design element. It comes in a wide variety of metals, including fine silver, sterling silver, gold-filled, gold, brass, copper, bronze, and steel. There are colored varieties and an assortment of sizes, called gauges, the thinnest having the highest number (30) and the thickest (10) being the heaviest. Malleability is the temper of the wire (from least to most flexible) and is described as full-hard, half-hard, and dead soft. Bending the wire repeatedly will work harden the metal, but too much bending will cause it to break.

Wireworking requires several types of pliers for wrapping and bending wire as desired. Flush cutters are also essential for cutting wire. See below for the description of the tools shown.

WIRE TOOLBOX

Wire Have wires in a variety of finishes and gauges at your disposal

Chain- and flat-nose pliers Use these types of pliers to manipulate wire and open and close jump rings. The inside jaws are flat and smooth on both types of pliers, but the outsides are different—chain-nose pliers are round and flat-nose pliers taper toward the tip *(A and B)*.

Flush cutters These sharp cutters create clean cuts when trimming wire to size or cutting off excess *(C and E)*.

Round-nose pliers Use these to make loops and curls in wire *(D)*.

Dowel rod Small dowel rods are used when creating jump rings or simple chains.

Butane torch Use to create a head pin from wire.

simple wireworking

{ Wire, beads, and pliers are essentially all you need to create a piece of jewelry. The following techniques are fundamental wireworking techniques used throughout this book.

WRAPPED LOOPS

1. Cut the wire 1¼" (3 cm) above the bead. Using chain-nose pliers, grasp the wire directly above the bead and bend the wire into a hook shape.

2. Hold the horizontal part of the wire with the pliers, close to the bend. Bend the wire over the top of the pliers, so the wire is horizontal in the other direction, forming the top of the loop.

3. Grab the top of the loop with the pliers and wrap the tail around the stem, covering it with wraps until it touches the bead.

4. For a tighter wrap, trim the excess and, using the pliers, flatten the trimmed wire to the stem. For a more decorative look, continue wrapping the tail around the stem, which will give it a knotted appearance.

*note TO MAKE DANGLES, USE EITHER A BALL OR REGULAR HEAD PIN. JUST ADD BEADS TO HEAD PINS AND COMPLETE USING WRAPPED-LOOP INSTRUCTIONS.

JUMP RINGS

1. Wrap wire around a dowel rod until a tight coil is formed.

2. Remove the coil by sliding it off of the dowel rod.

3. Separate the coils by snipping down the center with flush cutters or a jump ringer.

4. If desired, fuse the open ends of the links with a butane torch.

*note RECYCLE! SCRAP CURVES FROM THE CUT COIL CAN BE MADE INTO BUTTON SHANKS.

The width of the dowel will determine the circumference of the jump rings. Wrap tight enough so that the coil stays snug on the dowel but not so tight that it cannot be removed.

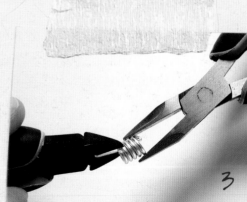

3

wire

FINE SILVER FUSED CHAIN

1. Wrap the wire uniformly and snuggly around a dowel rod to determine the size of the links. Remove the coil from the rod and use flush cutters to trim off the jump rings.

2. Using a butane torch, fuse the opening of half of the rings by applying even heat to the area until it glows slightly and flows together (caution: too much heat and the piece will slump). Also, the ends must fit flush together or the metal won't fuse closed.

3. Form a chain by interlocking the fused links and those that are still open. Then make sure the rings are closed firmly and fuse the rest.

4. The fine silver chain is very malleable at this stage and can be altered by using round-nose pliers to gently open the link and shape it into an oval, or it can be hammered to add texture.

*note STAINLESS STEEL WIRE IS ALREADY HARDENED + WON'T BREAK APART. IT IS A HARD WIRE TO WORK WITH + REQUIRES HEAVY-DUTY TOOLS.

DRAWING A BEAD

Silver wire, when heated, will redden and draw in on itself. Then the molten silver will form a ball.

This is called "drawing a bead" and is a decorative way to make head pins or draw both ends into beads to loop together and make a chain. A small butane torch, pliers, either fine or sterling silver wire, and a heat-proof surface are all you need. See page 125 for more detailed instructions.

HEAD PINS

1. Cut wire to desired length, leaving about ¼" (6.35 mm) extra to create the tip of the head pin (more if you wish to have a larger tip).

2. Hold the wire vertically with a set of pliers and heat the tip with a torch. Adjust the flame to medium until it forms a tight brush shape.

3. Place the tip into the flame so that it is about ¼" (6.35 mm) away from the hot blue part of the flame. The wire will go dull, then reddish. Move the flame around the tip until the end draws up into a ball. Once it draws up, quickly remove the heat (be mindful that, as it heats, the end can become too heavy and fall off of the wire).

FANCY WIRE WRAP

1. Use a 5" (13 cm) length of wire to form a loop about 2" (5 cm) from the end of the wire. You will have a 1½" (4 cm) tail. Wrap the tail around the stem three times.

2. Add the bead.

3. Form another loop, starting ⅛" (3 mm) away from the bead.

4. Wrap the tail around the stem three times.

5. Repeat Steps 2 through 4 and continue wrapping the tails around the loops and tuck in the ends.

An amazingly versatile material, polymer clay is a modeling compound made from polyvinyl chloride (PVC) mixed with plasticizers to increase smoothness and workability. It is highly malleable in its uncured state and can be sculpted, extruded, and impressed with detailed textures. In its cured state, polymer clay is very durable and can be sanded, carved, and polished. Polymer clay is also available in many rich colors and textures, from pearlescent to stonelike. It comes in varying consistencies, such as lightweight or flexible. The best advantage to this material is how easy it is to use and the wide availability of polymer clays and equipment. All polymer clays must be cured in an oven, in a toaster oven, or with a heat gun.

polymer clay

Polymer clay should be stored so that it is protected from dust and lint. Lidded boxes will also protect it from direct sunlight, which will cause it to harden.

POLYMER CLAY TOOLBOX

Pasta machine This is available at any craft store and are used to roll out sheets or to condition the polymer clay. Do not use for food after running polymer clay through it.

Heat gun Regular heat guns are available at craft stores, but a paint stripper from the hardware store is a better choice. Opt for a model with two settings.

Toaster oven or oven An easy method to cure raw polymer, a toaster oven or an oven will provide more even heating during this stage than a heat gun will.

Ceramic tiles Purchase these in small sizes for making texture stamps on (see page 41); they are also a good work surface for polymer because the surface will grip the polymer. Plus, the ceramic is heat resistant.

Oven thermometer To get accurate temperature readings from your oven, use an oven thermometer for properly fired pieces.

Wooden tools These are used for shaping and sculpting, and the wood grain will grip the clay.

Spray bottles Fill one with water and another with rubbing alcohol. The water is a good resist for stamps and the alcohol is great for smoothing the surface of polymer clay by gently dissolving it.

Craft knife A knife and stash of sharp blades are useful to have on hand for trimming off excess pieces of clay.

Tissue blade A long, thin blade is good for slicing cane or trimming edges.

Sandpaper You should have wet and dry in various grits—350, 500, 600, and 2000. The lower the number, the coarser the grit. Use the rougher grits to remove excess material. Use the higher numbers to polish and buff. Work your way up from the rougher to finer, as this will take care of scratches to create a smooth surface.

Buffing cloth Twill or denim work well to shine the surface of cured polymer clay.

Buffing wheel If you have one, use it with a muslin wheel. It will polish cured polymer clay faster than hand polishing, leaving pieces incredibly shiny.

Metal dowels Use them when creating beads from polymer clay because the metal is heat resistant, and the smooth surface prevents the polymer clay from sticking to it.

Inclusions Glitter, pigment powders, bits of baked polymer clay, sand, foils, and any other heat-resistant item can be blended into polymer clay for wonderful custom pieces, interesting patterns, and great textures.

Storage containers Plastic or metal, lidded, and partitioned storage boxes keep polymer clay colors separate and free of dust and lint. Keep the polymer clay out of direct sunlight, otherwise it will harden and become difficult to condition.

types of polymer clay

SUPER SCULPEY A perfect clay for mold making and making masters (see pages 42–43), this clay is widely used throughout many fields as the choice for model makers. It has a pinkish tan color and is slightly stiff. This clay must be thoroughly conditioned to prevent brittleness after curing. Super Sculpey should be cured in a preheated oven at 275°F (135°C) for fifteen minutes per ¼" (6 mm) of thickness.

SCULPEY III The most common clay, it is available in several colors and finishes. It has a very soft texture, almost stretchy. Sculpey III should be cured in a preheated oven at 275°F (135°C) for fifteen minutes per ¼" (6 mm) of thickness.

PREMO! SCULPEY Harder to find, this clay is very richly pigmented and slightly firmer in texture. Premo! Sculpey should be cured in a preheated oven at 275°F (135°C) for thirty minutes per ¼" (6 mm) of thickness.

STUDIO BY SCULPEY This newer version of Sculpey is available in larger blocks, and the colors are more natural, almost muted. The texture is softer and lighter than Premo!. Some colors, such as reds, cure a little less hard. Studio by Sculpey should be cured in a preheated oven at 275°F (135°C) for thirty minutes.

CERNIT This polymer clay is more difficult to find in the United States. Doll makers use it because the flesh color has the appearance of porcelain. The colors are very rich and the polymer clay hardens perfectly. Cernit should be cured in a preheated oven at 265°F (129°C) for fifteen to thirty minutes.

LIQUID POLYMER There are a few brands, but it is more or less the same product. This useful goop can be tinted with pigments or used in its natural cloudy white state as glue for unbaked polymer clay. It can also be used as a transfer medium: apply to a printed image on paper, attach to the desired piece of polymer clay with another drop of liquid polymer, bake, then remove the excess paper by wetting and gently rubbing. The paper will come off, but the image will remain.

*note HANDLE WITH CARE! ALL RAW POLYMER CLAY CAN STAIN SURFACES, SUCH AS PLASTICS OR VARNISHED FURNITURE.

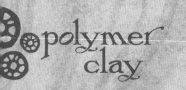

preparation

When properly cured, polymer clay is durable, waterproof, colorfast, and lightweight. Before working with it, read through the following tips for best results.

~ Keep area and hands clean; dust and oil will contaminate clay, giving it a grayish cast. Clean your hands with cleansing wipes between working with different colors of polymer clay to keep the clays clean.

~ Avoid wearing dark clothes because the fibers will adhere to the polymer clay and give it a linty quality that must be painted over or used as bead cores.

~ Always condition polymer clay before you use it, either by hand mixing or running it through the pasta machine. If it is too soft to work with, let it rest for a moment or throw it in the fridge. The cold temperature will stiffen the polymer clay.

~ To attach a core bead to a mandrel, make the bead/shape about half the size of the desired finished bead. Push through the mandrel, maintaining the shape, and press around the mandrel, securing it. Fire with the heat gun on the medium setting until the bead has a matte finish.

~ Color mixing is easy: just run polymer clay through the pasta machine or hand blend. To add powders, simply dent the clay, sprinkle a pinch of pigment into the depression, and fold over, blending it in. The color recipes that accompany each project in the next chapter are measured in ratios or parts and therefore can be mixed to create objects of any size.

A pasta machine can be used both to condition and to mix colors of clay.

*note TO CREATE UNIFORM BEADS, ROLL CONDITIONED CLAY INTO A LOG, PLACE ALONG A RULER + CUT TO ACHIEVE EQUAL AMOUNTS.

baking

It is best to dedicate a small toaster oven for polymer clay. If using an oven used also for food, tent aluminum foil over the pieces to prevent fumes from adhering to the interior of the oven. When baking, follow the manufacturer's instructions for specific temperatures and times. Purchase an oven thermometer to ensure the most accurate temperature. Keep an eye on the pieces to prevent them from burning, which releases toxic fumes. A heat gun can be used to bake small pieces or to cure liquid polymer. Keep the heat gun on a low setting and move in a circular motion to prevent scorching or bubbling. Underbaking polymer clay can cause cracks, due to the layers of raw clay expanding against the cured outer shell. Pieces ¼" (6 mm) thick should be baked in an oven. Polyester fiberfill is useful for baking polymer clay, because the cushioning minimizes impressions from glass or metal surfaces.

finishing

Polymer clay can be finished in numerous ways: buffed and sanded to a high shine, varnished with lacquer, or left in its natural matte. To enhance the texture of cured polymer clay, buff with a cloth. Denim and heavy twill work well. To hand polish, use wet and dry sandpaper, 500 grit and 2000 grit, respectively, for a nice shine. Make sure you dip the piece in water frequently to prevent dust. Coincidentally, the water and dust will mix to form its own buffing compound to prevent further scratches and to achieve an even brighter shin. To sand small, flat pieces, press a piece of rolled-up duct tape onto the back of the piece. This will give your fingers extra traction while sliding the piece across the sandpaper. If finishing with lacquer, spray in quick, even coats and set somewhere undisturbed to dry.

BUFFED

LACQUERED

PAINTED WITH ACRYLIC PAINT

WET SANDED TO A HIGH POLISH

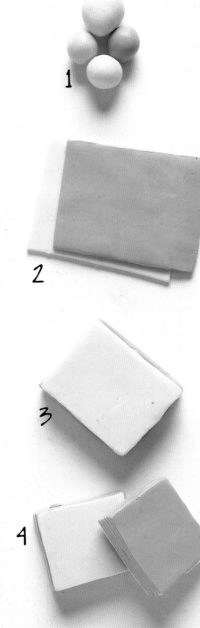

1

2

3

4

6

polymer techniques

Polymer clay is unique in that it can be made to look like wood, stone, metal, ceramic, and glass, as well as custom appearances. The following technique shows how to create faux ivory.

FAUX IVORY

Color recipe: cream (one part), tan (one part), white (one part), and translucent (two parts).

1. Mix the cream, tan, and white clays.

2. Use a pasta machine to create a sheet with the mixed clay and the translucent clay.

3. Trim the sheets into rectangles.

4. Create a stack with the sheets, alternating the colors.

5. Slice the block in half and stack again.

6. Gently reduce with your hands or a clay roller until you are satisfied with the grain.

7. Slice pieces from the edge of the stacks and fire. Once cool, coat with a wash of burnt amber acrylic, if desired.

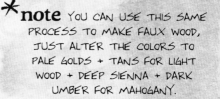

*note YOU CAN USE THIS SAME PROCESS TO MAKE FAUX WOOD, JUST ALTER THE COLORS TO PALE GOLDS + TANS FOR LIGHT WOOD + DEEP SIENNA + DARK UMBER FOR MAHOGANY.

precious metal clay

A revolutionary material, Precious Metal Clay (PMC) is as if ceramic stoneware clay married metalsmithing. It has many advantages: it can be sculpted, rolled into sheets, extruded, and made into a paste. It also can be erected to a hollow form and used to construct intricate shapes. But perhaps its best attribute is that it is easy to master with satisfying, not to mention fast, results. It dries out quickly, so it must be covered to maintain its plasticity. It is packaged in airtight bags, which should only be opened when ready to use. To retain moisture between uses, store clay wrapped in plastic in an airtight container with a moist paper towel in the refrigerator until the next use. Make sure the paper towel and clay do not touch!

The tools necessary for metal clay look as if they come from an apothecary's workshop. The specimen jar with wet sponge is used to keep metal clay from drying out during use.

METAL CLAY TOOLBOX

Plastic flexible cutting boards Lay these over your work surface to provide a nonstick work area, protect your table, and allow easy mobility of metal clay pieces. They are also good to scrape down and funnel dry clay into a slip jar.

Tissue blades Long, slim blades are good for cutting sheets of metal clay.

Olive oil Cover your hands, cutting board, and stamps (sparingly) with olive oil to prevent the metal clay from sticking to them. Too much olive oil will break down the clay.

Beeswax and shielding lotion These prevent the metal clay from sticking to your hands. They also keep the clay from drying out and irritating your skin.

Bowl with sponge Metal clay must be moist; therefore, moisten tools with a sponge and water for best results.

Spray bottle with water Use to mist clay and keep it moist.

Slip jar Slip is metal clay and water mixed into a paste and is essential for attaching clay parts.

Paintbrushes (size 2 or 4) Utilize these for blending or adding water to dry areas and attaching pieces together.

Straws in various sizes Coffee stirrers cut down to 1" (2.5 cm) are perfect for making holes.

Variety of cutters Small cookie/candy cutters are perfect for cutting shapes from sheets of clay.

Heating plate or coffee warmer This heat source will quickly dry metal clay prior to firing.

Cork clay Imported from Japan, this type of clay (made from a mixture of cork and cellulose) is necessary to create hollow forms. It will burn away when the metal clay is fired in a kiln.

Playing cards or matte board You can use these to measure the rolling thicknesses of clay.

Roller This tool is excellent for making sheets of metal clay.

Nail files Have these handy in various grits for sanding small areas of bone-dry pieces.

Ring mandrel You will need this tool for shaping ring shanks.

Liver of sulfur This is needed to create a patina finish (see pages 35–37 for more details).

Container for clay Use a plastic cup, cloche, or small ceramic pot or bowl to cover clay and keep it fresh.

Kiln To properly fire metal clay, it will be necessary to have a kiln that can reach 1,650°F (899°C) and hold this temperature for two hours.

Brass brush or tumbler with steel shot pellets These items are necessary to properly work harden metal.

25

types of metal clay

Standard PMC shrinks about 30 percent, and thinner items may shrink more. It is more porous and therefore not as strong as the denser formulas. Standard PMC is perfect for making detailed masters, which are used to create a mold (see pages 42–43), because you can work larger and the detail will tighten up as it shrinks.

PMC Plus has a 12 to 15 percent shrinkage rate and a lower firing time (but it may not fully sinter at the lower temperature, so fire at 1,650°F [899°C]).

PMC 3 seems to shrink the least, at 10 percent, and is the strongest formula due to its density. It also has the shortest firing temperature; small, thin pieces can be fired with a butane torch. This clay is perfect for making rings and bails, or any-where extra strength is desired. All the projects in this book are made with PMC 3.

These charms are all made from metal clay. Small balls of clay were pressed into handmade stamps, fired, and then finished in a tumbler. The various colors were produced with liver of sulfur.

sintering

Metal clay is metal (silver, gold, bronze, or copper) particles mixed in an organic binder, which burns away in a kiln, leaving only the sintered metal behind. Sintering is the process of creating solid objects by heating particles or powders until they adhere to one another. Therefore, to achieve ideal results, it is important to re-member that pieces must be fired in a kiln to fully sinter the metal and that the metal must be work hardened (by tumbling with steel shot, by burnishing with a brass brush, or by hammering). This lessens the inherent porosity.

working with metal clay

Fresh clay is easiest to work with and is very mold-able. This moist clay will be slightly cool to the touch (temperature is a good way of telling how fresh and moist your clay is). Use fresh clay for making sheets (roll a piece between two strips of matte board or craft sticks for consistent thickness throughout the sheets), pressing into stamps, rolling into logs, rolling into balls, sculpting, texturing, cutting with cutters, or poking holes in with straws. To maintain working time, the clay must be periodically hydrated. Do not overwet the clay or it will break down and turn into a slurry.

Bone-dry clay is completely devoid of all moisture and therefore maintains its shape. Bone-dry clay will be at room temperature. Use this for building forms, such as a box. You can sand it with various grits of sandpaper, carve it with a knife or engraving tools, burnish it, or wet it with a brush to make a slurry and attach other dry pieces. It is much easier to attach two dry compo-nents rather than trying to apply a wet bail to a pendant. It is also much easier to make repairs and apply finishing techniques in this stage, rather than after firing when the clay has sintered. Use the warming plate to speed drying time and get the clay bone dry. Clean up the piece by sanding all of the edges or use a wet paintbrush to smooth around the perimeter of holes so they aren't jagged. The more finishing that is completed in this stage, the less work later.

If the clay hardens into an undesirable shape, don't throw it away! Grind it with a mortar and pestle or chop it into a powder and add it to the slip jar (wear a dust mask to prevent inhalation). It can also be ground with a small amount of water to create a thick paste, which should then sit out until it is malleable. Dried and rehydrated clay is never as easy to work with as fresh clay, due to the grainy texture, but it should never be thrown away.

Metal clay should be tumbled after firing to work harden the metal. The top chain has been tumbled and patinaed (see pages 35–37 for more details). The middle chain was tumbled and the bottom chain is straight out of the kiln without any finishing.

firing

Without proper attention to the firing process, brittle and subpar pieces will result. Start with a cold kiln (adding pieces to a preheated kiln can cause bubbling or odd surface defects). Ramping the kiln to temperature also allows any unknown moisture to evaporate.

No pieces should be touching—lay pieces in a single layer on a firebrick, vermiculite, or investment powder. These provide cushioning or support for more intricate shapes, and in the case of firebrick, will improve mobility of the fired pieces. For most metal clay firing, you'll use the firebrick. Vermiculite and investment should only be used when necessary, as they're difficult to clean up. The vermiculite in particular is tricky because if the metal pieces you are firing "super heat," it can cause a dimpled surface on the clay it is touching. This is

rare, but it sometimes happens, especially on older, non-digital kilns.

The firebricks are also good to keep the pieces from direct contact with the interior of the kiln, which could have fluctuations in firing temperatures. Firebricks can also be used to keep pieces standing upright. This is particularly helpful when making fused fine silver chain.

Investment powder is normally used in casting. For the purposes in this book, it provides a pillowy cushion for hollow forms to rest in (see Magpie Pendant on pages 134–135). This prevents the metal from flattening on one side and keeps the shape of the metal clay piece. The same theory applies for vermiculite. It won't burn off in the kiln.

Fire the kiln outside, protected from the elements, or in a well-ventilated area so you don't inhale fumes. Once the kiln reaches temperature, fire completely for two hours. Many claim that you can fire small items made out of the "quick fire" clays for ten minutes with a torch, but this can result in brittle, half-sintered pieces. They can break, revealing the chalky interior. Fire for two hours for fully sintered metal. There is no reason not to—if you spent time making your piece, fire it properly so it lasts.

*note ADDING METAL CLAY PIECES TO A HOT KILN MIGHT MAKE THEM EXPLODE, ESPECIALLY IF THEY ARE NOT COMPLETELY DRY.

repairing sintered metal

After firing, if there are flaws in the piece, such as cracks, you can fix them with slip or patch them with clay. If you are going to make repairs, don't polish the piece. Leave it rough so the slip can bond properly. If it looks thin, or if the crack is still visible, apply another layer. Allow the slip to dry and fire fully again. Or use a small butane torch and a heatproof surface (such as a firebrick or soldering plate) to heat

the piece if it's a minute repair or a very thin, small piece. At first a little smoke will come off the piece; this is the organic binder burning off. Continue to heat in a circular motion until it's cherry red and hold for about a minute, then let it cool. This works for pieces that aren't designed for lots of wear and tear, such as decorative embellishments, but it is not recommended for hinges or a toggle bar.

simple metal clay findings

{ Create your own custom metallic jewelry findings so that your finished piece will be unique, from the foundation to the centerpiece.

TOGGLE CLASP

1. Roll out a sheet of metal clay to the desired thickness (thinner is more difficult to handle, so start with the thickness of matte board) on a texture stamp or card (see page 40 for instructions).

2. Remove the center of the clasp with a clay cutter. Cut out the middle with a smaller cutter.

3. Poke a hole with a stir stick or needle tool for the beading wire to pass through.

4. Cut out a bar from the sheet of clay, making sure the width is small enough to fit through the hole in the clasp and the length is longer than the width of the hole—too short of a bar and the clasp will not hold; too long and it will be difficult to clasp. Then poke a hole in the center of the bar for the beading wire to pass through.

5. Place both pieces on the warming plate. Once dry, test to see whether the pieces fit together. If not, alter to fit properly, or make another set with the new pieces designed to fit with the first set.

6. Finish the dry clay by sanding or using a wet brush and finger to smooth the edges. Fire, cool, and finish.

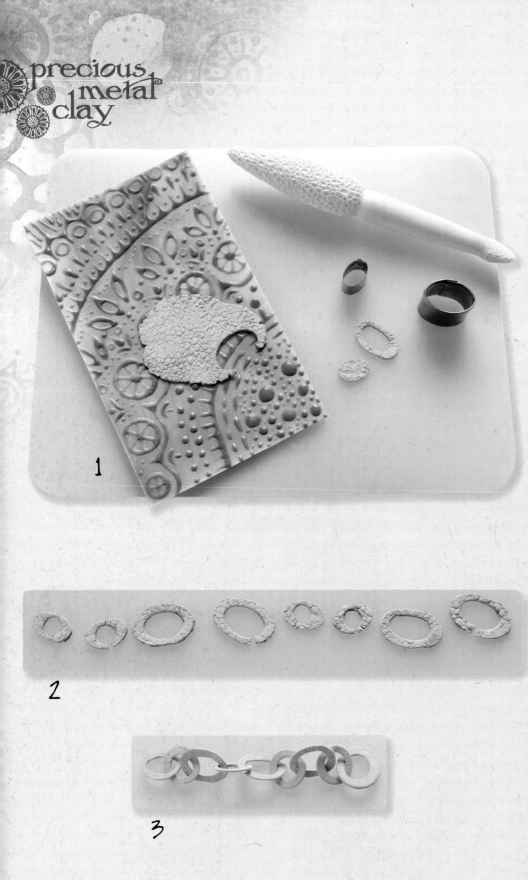

1

2

3

CHAIN

1. Roll out a sheet of metal clay to medium thickness between two texture cards or stamps (see pages 40–41 for instructions), so both sides are textured. Use a clay cutter to cut out the link shapes and remove the centers.

2. Place the links on a warming plate. When leather-hard, remove. (Leather-hard is a term that describes the state of the clay in proportion to the amount of moisture left in the clay. It means specifically that the clay is cool to the touch, holds its shape, and feels flexible like leather.) Cut a slit through every other link.

3. To create the chain, carefully open a link and insert another link. Close using slip to conceal the cut. Continue until all of the links are used. Check all links and repair any cracks before firing.

4. Fire and cool. Links will probably be stuck together; simply twist the chain to loosen. If some links look misshapen, use pliers to straighten them out before tumbling.

BUTTON

1. Roll out a ball of metal clay and press into the middle of a texture stamp (see page 41 for instructions). Pull the clay away to check the quality. If the desired definition is achieved, lay it on the warming plate.

2. Roll out a small ball of clay about the size of a small pea. Flatten and then poke a hole through the center with a coffee stirrer. Cut the resulting ring in half and allow to dry.

3. Use slip to attach the half circle to the back of the button, moving the half circle until it grabs. Brush a little slip around the seam and allow to dry.

4. Fire, cool, and finish.

1

2

3

setting stones {

There are many ways to set stones in metal clay. You can set vintage glass cabochons (bezel wire), opal cabochons (prong set), or even delicate pearls (bezel cups). Synthetic stones are amazing with metal clay because they can be fired with it (they are designed to withstand high temperatures). These are easily set in any of the listed methods, but are especially useful in ball settings. Stones not designed for high temperatures will crack or melt.

Prong setting is perfect for mounting delicate stones and specimens that wouldn't survive in the kiln. This piece uses a prong set with a hollow form (see pages 134–135 for complete project).

PRONG SET

This is an unusual setting for large natural stones or specimens. Use thick, fine silver wire, ball the ends (see page 18), and trim so that it is long enough to hold the stone and also to set into the metal clay base. Rough up the cut ends of wire with coarse sandpaper to help them grab the clay and remain secure. Press the wire, cut side first, into the clay base, until it reaches the other side (don't worry if the wire pops through the other side—after firing, the tips sticking out can be cut with flush cutters and burnished down). Arrange the prongs so that the stone fits loosely to accommodate for shrinkage. It is better for the prongs to be a touch large than too small. Allow the base to dry. Apply a coat of slip to the bases of the wire for stability. Add another coat if it looks weak or if there are cracks. The slip will fuse to the wire and the metal clay base. Make sure the prongs are set well into the clay and reinforced with slip. Dry and fire. Place the stone between the prongs and close them snuggly, so the stone doesn't wiggle. Burnish the prongs with a burnishing tool to harden them. Finish the rest of the piece.

BEZELS

Bezels are used to set stones. They are essentially cups that stones are placed inside. There are several techniques for creating bezels. The two shown here each have a similar appearance. The type of stone you wish to set in metal clay will determine the best technique to use.

CLAY BALL + BEZEL CUPS

These two techniques are essentially the same—the difference again lies in the type of stone you are setting. The clay ball technique is great when you are using synthetic stones that can withstand the heat of the kiln. Bezel cups are good for stones that are not able to go into the kiln. Use fine silver cups that fit the stones. Press the cups into the surface of the metal clay, using a tool or brush to blend slip into the seam. Allow the piece to dry. Fire, then drop the stone in, press the edge down with a tool, and smooth down. Polish to the desired finish. See the steps below for an idea of how to accomplish both.

1

CLAY BALL

1. Roll out a ball of metal clay. Use either a straw or tool to make a hole a little larger than the stone.

2. Using tweezers, drop the stone into the ball, and close the sides of the ball around the stone.

2

precious metal clay

This technique is perfect for setting resin or fragile stones. Essentially, you are creating a cup from a length of bezel wire and a base of metal clay. Once you fire the cup, you can simply drop in the stone, gently bending the top edge of the bezel wire to hold the stone in place.

BEZEL WIRE

1. Measure the circumference of the stone by wrapping a strip of paper around it.

2. Use the paper to measure a length of fine silver bezel wire and cut to size.

3. Shape around a ring mandrel to get a perfect circle. Make sure that the ends meet flush and then use slip to coat the seam.

4. Roll out a sheet of metal clay to create the base of the cup. Texture as desired.

5. Press the bezel wire into the base of the metal clay and then apply a coat of slip around the bezel, both inside and out. Allow to dry, then fire. Drop the stone in and press down the bezel edges with a burnishing tool or wooden tool to hold the stone. Finish the piece by hand (if the stone is fragile) or by tumbling.

*note IF METAL CLAY GETS ON THE STONE, USE A PAINTBRUSH WITH WATER TO LIGHTLY CLEAN IT, OR ALLOW IT TO DRY, THEN SCRAPE IT OFF WITH A PIECE OF SANDPAPER FOLDED TO A POINT.

3

4

5

finishing

Metal clay can be tumbled, brushed with a brass brush, or polished with polishing pads on a Dremel, Foredoom, or other flexible-shaft rotary power tool. Tumbling is the easiest, and it also work hardens the metal so it isn't brittle. Any run-of-the-mill rock tumbler will work. Add a drop of dish soap to the water and 1 pound (455 g) of reusable stainless steel shot. The water should just barely cover the steel shot. Thread the pieces loosely onto a wire (if there are many) and twist closed. This step reduces the time spent digging through the shot. Allow pieces to tumble for about an hour and check the surface (differences in shot, the quantity of items in the tumbler, the soap, etc., can affect tumbling times). The pieces should be slightly shiny, but not completely bright. Remove and apply patina and then return to the tumbler. It can take anywhere from another hour to two or more, so check periodically until you achieve the desired finish. For a satin finish, briskly scrub tumbled or nontumbled pieces with a brass brush and soap. If using polishing heads on a Dremel, be careful not to apply too much pressure, which can mark up the surface.

adding color to metal clay pieces

{ There are many ways to add color to metal, including patinas, enamels, colored epoxy resin, acrylic paint, and colored pencils. These are methods to embellish the surface of metal clay when stones are not used as focal points. This section will address patinas, acrylic paints, and colored pencils.

PATINA

Patina is the oxidation of the metal's surface, a way of coloring that is ephemeral and changing. Liver of sulfur is the most common and easiest way to color silver but is also the most unpredictable. Experiment with variations of finished silver, from white and unprepared to brushed and tumbled. The effects here are achieved on slightly tumbled pieces, so that the patina adheres to the remaining silver oxide and the maximum detail is brought out.

*note DEPENDING ON THE FRESHNESS + POTENCY OF THE LIVER OF SULFUR, MORE MAY NEED TO BE ADDED AS NECESSARY. SIGNS OF FRESHNESS INCLUDE A STRONG ODOR THAT SMELLS LIKE ROTTEN EGGS + A BRIGHT YELLOW-GREEN COLOR.

PATINA FINISH

1. To prepare the solution, dissolve a pea-size chunk of liver of sulfur in warm to hot water contained in glass or plastic (do not use containers made from reactive metals, such as copper or aluminum). The hotter the water, the faster the color change. Also, make sure that the chunks completely dissolve. Otherwise, the small bits will stick to your piece, and your patina will be uneven and spotted. The solution should be bright yellow-green. Have a jar of clean, cold water ready to rinse and stop the reaction of the chemical.

2. Rinse the piece in warm water and soap to remove oil and residue.

3. Dip the piece (using nonreactive tongs, a tea ball, or wire) into the solution and swirl for a few seconds. Remove. The oxygen in the air will react with the liver of sulfur, and the piece will start changing color. Repeat as necessary to achieve the desired color.

4. Quickly dip the piece into cold water to stop the process. When you reach the desired effect, wash with dish soap to stop the reaction completely.

5. As it is worn, the surface will alter, mellowing over time or darkening. To preserve a patina on the surface of the metal, spray with a light coat of varnish or clear aerosol polyurethane. Make sure the spray can tip is at least 12" (30.5 cm) away from the piece and that you make even passes with the can.

Depending on how long you dip pieces in liver of sulfur, you can achieve a patina in a range of colors, from gold to black. The colors will go from gold to rose, violet, blue, brown, and finally black. Examine the color—if you want more color, repeat dipping and rinsing. For a deeper rose/violet, add one drop of ammonia; for a deeper blue, add two drops of ammonia; for a deeper brown, add ¼ teaspoon of baking soda.

ACRYLICS & COLORED PENCILS

Acrylics can be used in small amounts and in places where the color won't see a lot of rubbing, such as inside crevices or within a bezel. The paint will resist on a polished surface; therefore, polished metal will need to be roughed up with sandpaper so the paint will have a toothy surface on which to adhere. This surface can also be primed with white absorbent acrylic gesso, for richer color. The same method for prepping can be used for colored pencils as well, just seal finished work thoroughly with a varnish spray.

This piece shows how beautiful the technique of painting on metal clay can look.
ARTIST Candace Wakumoto

The tools and textures described on the next few pages can be used on either polymer clay or Precious Metal Clay; the only difference is the resist used to keep tools and clays from sticking (use water for polymer and olive oil for Precious Metal Clay). The tools and textures are simple to make and will set your work apart because they are completely unique. These useful items will replace generic rubber stamps and ceramic tools, so get ready to fill your toolbox!

texturing clay

simple carving & sculpting tools

Tools for sculpting and carving are easy to come by. You can pick up tools from hobby and craft shops, ceramic supply stores, and dentist supply stores (implements fashioned to get into the nooks and crannies of your teeth are perfect for sculpting little masterpieces). Hobby and craft shops and ceramic supply stores will offer generic spoon tools in the ever-present boxwood variety. But tools that are perfect, that do exactly the job you want, can be made with little effort. For working with polymer clay, customized cuticle sticks and hardwood toothpicks are great because the wood has just enough texture to grab the clay. They are easy to customize for different needs (for example, creating those specific tools for carving text or scooping clay out of reverse texture stamps). African porcupine quills (naturally shed, of course) are perfect for metal clay because of their smoother, water-resistant surface.

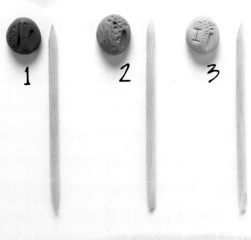

1   2   3

African porcupine quills are perfect for adding perfect detail to metal clay and polymer clay.

SCULPTING TOOLS

1. Begin by gently shaving off the stick until you have a useful shape (for example, squared off point, rounded wedge, sharp point, and variations of the wedge in different widths).

2. Use the sandpaper to further enhance the shape.

3. Use a buffing block, coarsest to high shine, polishing until the tool tip is perfectly smooth, no splinters or bumps.

4. Brand them with a permanent marker (because your artist buddies will steal them).

This ivory texture tool is designed to texture dimensional surfaces, flat areas, and recessed spaces that would be impossible to reach with a rubber stamp.

simple texture tools

Textures are a fine addition to any project. Use them to highlight a focal point, as an interesting accent, or on their own. Unique textures will keep your work exciting and completely your own. Shown above is an ivory tool used for texturing and handmade texture pads created from silicone rubber. You can use two-part silicone putty (available from jewelry supply shops) to make all sorts of useful and flexible texture pads. Mix the two parts right before you are ready to make the texture pad because it sets up quickly. These are fun to make, so go on a texture expedition! Look for rocks, fruit (citrus fruits and melons work well), leaves, bark, fabric, cement sidewalks, the bottom of your foot—basically, anything with an interesting texture. Usually, silicone putties have mold releases built in so you don't have to worry about them sticking, but if not, use a release recommended by the manufacturer.

RUBBER TEXTURE PADS

1. Roll the putty into a ball after mixing thoroughly (color is uniform when mixed) and press into the center of the texture, pressing into a thin layer to prevent air pockets.

2. Wait until it hardens, then remove slowly. If it sticks, let it sit longer. Silicones can set anywhere from five minutes to an hour, so check the label.

texture cards

This technique is great for rolling out sheets of textured metal clay to use to build boxes, bezels, ring shanks, and pendants. These sheets can also be reversed by running through a pasta machine with a sheet of polymer clay and then baked to create a reverse texture card.

TEXTURE CARD + STAMP

1. Begin by mixing two batches of liquid polymer with pigment powders in small bowls (about a tablespoon of liquid polymer and one scoop of pigment powder from the end of a cuticle stick per bowl). Mix until smooth. Coat one side of the index card with a thick layer of liquid polymer and cure with a heat gun set on medium. The polymer goes translucent when it is cured, allowing the pigment powder to shine. Allow the sheet to cool. Using a wooden tool, apply the alternate color of polymer to the card in a pattern.

2. Working in segments to prevent smudging the pattern, cure the polymer with a heat gun. If you use an oven, the heat from the oven will cause the pattern to spread. Therefore, use the heat gun to quickly cure a skin over the drops, allowing them to maintain their shape and not flatten out, as they would in the oven.

3. Continue layering the pattern onto the card, even building on top of cured patterns. This technique can be as richly detailed as desired.

4. Use the texture to press into a ball of polymer, creating a texture stamp.

5. To make a reverse of the pattern, run the card through a pasta machine with a sheet of polymer clay on a thick setting using water or powder on the liquid polymer patterned sheet as a resist. Trim the polymer clay sheet to size and cure in the oven according to the manufacturer's instructions.

reverse texture stamps

This is a texture technique that is so useful, addictive, and gratifying that making one stamp simply won't be enough. These little gems can be used on any clay medium (stoneware, porcelain, paper clay, springerle dough, butter, metal clay, and polymer clay), although using them on marzipan (yes, marzipan is considered a clay) after having stamped out goods in metal clay or any other nonedible material is inadvisable. Make several because they will come in handy.

Remember: Deeper marks will be raised and come to the forefront, and shallower marks will be background textures. This method is good for text because it allows tight detail. To press goods from polymer clay, brush the stamp with water or dust with cornstarch, which will act as a resist, keeping the polymer clay from sticking to the stamp. To press goods from metal clay, brush the stamp with a light coat of olive oil, being sure to get into the details.

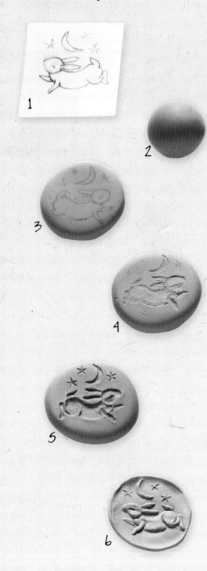

CREATING REVERSE TEXTURE STAMPS

1. Draw or trace an image with graphite to use to create the stamp.

2. Roll out a ball of conditioned polymer clay, as large as you wish the stamp to be, but if you are working with metal clay, make it larger because metal clay shrinks. Press the ball of polymer clay onto a ceramic tile to flatten it to $^3/_8$" (1 cm) thickness.

3. Position your image on the flattened clay and transfer by applying light pressure. Remove the paper and let the polymer rest in the fridge if it is too soft. The cold temperature will stiffen up the polymer clay.

4. Using a wooden cuticle tool, scrape around the contours of the design, working from the perimeter to the middle. Scoop more polymer clay from the areas that are raised, less from where the design is recessed.

5. Cure with a heat gun set on medium, constantly moving the heat around to keep from burning the polymer clay. Once cool, flip the polymer clay disc and carve the other side—waste not, want not!

6. Cure completely according to the manufacturer's instructions (most clay needs fifteen minutes for every ¼" [6.4 mm] at 275°F [135°C]). If you use the oven for food, tent a piece of foil over the stamp (the fumes will adhere to the foil and not the oven) and turn on the vent. Use the stamp to press into clay.

molds

↠ This skill is incredibly useful. The ability to make multiple copies of a single piece is not just gratifying but also lucrative and time-saving. The materials are easy to use but require patience and time. Do not begin a mold if you don't have time to finish it. An experienced mold maker will spend about two hours from start to finish. This includes time to set up, mix, pour, clean up, and watch that the mold doesn't leak before it sets. ↞

MOLD-MAKING TOOLBOX

Plastilene clay (nonhardening clay found at craft stores)

Piece of plywood

Tissue blade or ruler

Wooden tools

Cardboard tube or plastic cup

Silicone rubber

Stir sticks

Clean plastic cups with ridges

Mold release

prep the master

Begin by examining the master, which is the item to be molded. Look for a spot or an area with the largest mass. This is where you want your pour spout to go. This is so the weight of the resin can use gravity and force resin into little nooks and crannies. Also, if it is in a larger area, the pour hole can be larger. If you pour resin from a small, narrow tube, the resin will back up from the air pocket formed by the larger space inside and possibly even set up before the mold cavity is filled. Check for undercuts and set the piece on the table, resting on the pour spout. Look for pieces that jut out or point toward the table, forming the equivalent of a U-bend in plumbing; these spots are hard to fill in. If you have spots like this, try to adjust the pour spout accordingly.

Place the block of plastilene clay in the center of the piece of plywood. The piece of plywood will protect your work surface from drips or accidental leaks and allow more mobility of the mold. Press the block of plastilene clay down. Using your hands, smooth down the plastilene clay so that it is even and level. Make sure the surface area of the plastilene clay is larger than the largest circumference of the master and that the plastilene clay is at least ½" (1.3 cm) thick. To check if the plastilene clay is level, rake the edge of the tissue blade or a ruler across the surface, skimming off any bumps or irregularities. Gently press the master into the center of the plastilene clay where your pour hole is intended. It's important that the master be securely anchored to the plastilene clay, or your master could dislodge during pouring. Take care not to press too hard, though; the

more of the master that is embedded in the plastilene clay, the larger the pour hole will be and the more the copies will need to be repaired.

Using your wooden tool, carefully seal the seam between the master and the plastilene clay. The goal is to seal any cracks where air bubbles might form. The master should meet the surface of the plastilene clay perpendicularly. If it doesn't and the seam was overly filled in and slopes, a lip will form on the copies and will need to be cleaned off later.

Place the cardboard tube over the master. Make sure the master does not touch the sides of the cardboard tube. If you use a cup, trim the bottom off and turn it over the master. Press firmly until the cardboard tube or bottomless cup is embedded in the plastilene clay at least halfway. Clean up and smooth over the seams along the bottom of the cardboard tube or cup where it meets the plastilene clay.

Alternatively, the sides can be built up using plastilene clay to create a box without a top. This is harder, though, because there are more seams to consider where there might be possible leaks. Also, depending on the size of the mold, the plastilene walls will need to be shored up so that they don't shift or collapse.

Once the master is created, it is time to create the mold. The mold will be created from silicone rubber, which must be precisely measured and poured to ensure a flawless mold that will be able to be used again and again.

EGG-SHAPED MASTER

1. Roll a ball of conditioned clay.

2. Use your fingers to taper one end into an egg and continue pulling one end to form a point. Smooth out with your fingers and fire.

3. Once cool, use a progression of 200- to 2000-grit sandpaper to smooth and polish. The master shown here sits atop a block of plastilene clay.

pour tips

Creating a perfect mold starts with proper pouring. Silicone rubber is created from two solutions. Pour each into its own clean, dry cup. Measure EXACTLY. This is important. Read all the directions on the label. Rubber can have different ratios and has to be exact to set up properly. If you don't have a scale, don't get rubber that needs to be weighed because the catalyst solution probably weighs more or less than the base side. If you eyeball it, it will be a nightmare to clean liquid rubber off your piece to be molded, not to mention a waste of the rubber! Use rubber that measures by volume, then you can mark the sides of the cups to fill accurately.

Pour the catalyst into the base, stirring gently as you pour. Mix thoroughly but do not whip the rubber into a bubbly froth. Mix it as if it were cake batter, gently and thoroughly, so it is smooth. Look to see whether there are any streaks of unmixed rubber in the mix. If so, keep mixing. Frequently tap the bowl on the table to dislodge any bubbles.

Pour the rubber in a high and steady thin stream into a corner of the mold away from the master (this eliminates bubbles), allowing it to fill around the bottom of the master first and work its way to the top. If you pour right on top of the master, you risk trapping air bubbles on the surface inside crevices. Fill the mold box until the rubber reaches ¼" (6.4 mm) above the master and tap lightly to dislodge any bubbles.

SILICONE MOLD

1. Cut a block of plastilene clay in half and smooth out lines with your fingers. Place the master in the middle of the clay block. Make sure the master is secure by gently pushing it into place. Cut a cardboard tube (a paper towel roll works great) so that it fits over the master with a 1" (2.5 cm) clearance.

2. Gently push the cardboard tube into the clay block to form a tight seal around the master. Dust the cavity with talc powder. Mix the silicone catalyst and base and pour into the cardboard tube. To reduce the occurrence of air bubbles, pour from a high angle so that the cavity fills slowly. Allow the silicone to set up (about seventeen hours). If it is tacky on top, it still needs time to set up.

3. Peel away the cardboard to reveal the mold. To release the master, carefully cut the silicone in a zigzag fashion. A straight cut will not allow the mold to line up perfectly for successive pours.

1

2

curing

Allow the rubber to cure on a level and undisturbed surface. It should stiffen in about an hour, but won't be ready to de-mold for about seventeen hours. Watch the mold and examine for leaks. If you see a tiny bit of rubber emerging from a crack, use clay to close it. That tiny stream can leak the whole mold, leaving a mess behind and an empty mold. To remove the master from the cured silicone rubber, first lift the mold off the plastilene clay base and then peel away the walls of cardboard tube, bottomless plastic cup, or plastilene clay walls, exposing the pour spout.

Use a craft knife to cut the rubber in a tight sawing fashion, cutting carefully along a side of the mold that is relatively detail free. Don't cut a seam right across a face or other hard-to-fix area. The cut should be jagged, which will serve as registration marks so the cut mold will line up exactly when you fill it with resin. If you make too straight and slick a cut, it is more likely the sides will move, resulting in resin leaks. Remove the master and spray with mold release. Allow to dry and then use a heavy rubber band to hold the mold closed. It is now ready to fill with resin!

resin

Resin is a magical material with three finished forms—clear as glass, translucent like frosted glass, and opaque. Resin can be molded, used as a coating, or carved like stone. It can also encapsulate objects, preserving them forever, like amber. The concept is akin to reliquaries, objects that hold and preserve the sacred remains of saints for eternity. The material is also easy to use, readily available, and inexpensive. Any brand is fine, but EnviroTex Light is a good option for its clarity, nonyellowing agents, and smaller bottles, which makes it easier to pour accurate measurements.

preparation

Working with resin requires a dust-free area with good ventilation. Turn off fans while pouring so that they do not kick up dust. Cover your work area with wax paper or newspaper to protect from spills and wear well-fitting gloves. Do not attempt to pour resin in poor lighting or if you are tired—you won't see imperfections. If molds have been sitting out for a long time, clean them with rubbing alcohol.

RESIN TOOLBOX

Resin solutions

Adjustable task lamp

Deep plastic lid

Butane torch

Clear packing tape

Craft sticks

Plastic cups with ridges

Resin dyes

Inclusions (pigment powders, glitter, leaves, sand, any dry particles)

Sandpaper for finishing

Rubber gloves

pour tips

Some resins are measured by weight and require a scale. Don't guess—unset resin is difficult to remove. When using a bezel, if resin is still tacky or doesn't set up at all, Attack! will chemically dissolve the resin overnight (place elements in a glass jar with a tight-fitting lid). If the resin doesn't set up in a mold, scoop it out and use alcohol to remove the residue.

Identical cups can be used to measure volume. Plastic cups with ridges make measuring easier—the ridges can serve as markers. Pour the contents from both cups into a third cup. Mix carefully and avoid whipping the mixture into a froth, scraping the sides and bottom. Mix properly or it won't cure; this usually takes two minutes or longer. Continue to mix if the resin looks streaky or cloudy. Carefully pour the mixture into a mold (see page 43 for more information) or bezel, allowing the resin to gradually fill the space from the lowest point to the top. Do not hastily dump it in right on top of the item you are encapsulating in a thick lump. This traps air and forms bubbles. Let the gravity of the resin force the bubbles up to the surface.

After the cavity is filled, inspect for bubbles. Surface bubbles can be removed with a light graze from a butane torch. A quick pass will force the bubbles to pop. Be careful not to let your torch linger or you could burn the resin and cause it to bubble up and blacken. Your breath works in a pinch, but do not inhale the resin fumes. A heat gun works, but the resin gets blown around, and it stirs up dust. Deep bubbles can be removed by gingerly popping with a pin, but don't try this if the resin has begun to set up because it will ruin the surface and possibly damage inclusions. If drips form, clean them off before the resin cures because it is much more difficult to scrape them off once they have hardened.

Cover the uncured resin with a deep lid or an overturned plastic container and set under a light. The heat will help it set faster. Allow the resin to set up overnight.

INCLUSIONS

If you wish to encapsulate items in resin, they should be dry and nonporous; otherwise, bubbles may form. Seal the pieces with gel medium to ensure this. To float an item in the middle, a base layer of resin must first be poured and allowed to harden somewhat before adding the item. Things tend to settle at the bottom—pour the first layer to ensure a centered piece. When the first layer is almost set, introduce the piece with a little pressure. Top off with more resin.

note METALLIC FLAKES ARE EXCELLENT INCLUSIONS WHEN CREATING WITH RESIN. BOTANICALS, SMALL GEMSTONES, OR POLYMER SCULPTURES ARE ALSO OPTIONS.

DYES

Resin dyes and powdered pigments can be added to the "B" solution prior to mixing. Use sparingly— too much dye can result in uncured resin. Tint a drop at time. Powders are less prone to reacting with the catalyst, and they can be added liberally. The dyes and powders can also be added before pouring if a swirl effect is desired, but remember not to add too much dye.

RESIN PENDANT

1. Set up your workspace—protect your work surface by taping wax paper to it and gather the following: three plastic cups, three stir sticks, inclusions, blazer torch, and a cover to protect the resin. Clean molds with rubbing alcohol to remove dust and allow to dry completely.

2. Pour resin parts A and B into two identical clean, dry plastic cups to ensure equal volumes. Using a scraping motion, mix the solutions together into a third cup. Be sure to mix slowly and steadily to avoid froth. Mix completely to reach an even color and consistency.

3. Slowly pour the solution into the form using a steady stream.

4. Use a butane torch or match to lightly and quickly graze the top of the resin to release any air bubbles. For troublesome bubbles, you can gently push a needle through the resin to pop them.

5. Cover the form with a lid to protect from dust. Allow the resin to set up for about eight hours under a lamp. For the first thirty minutes of setup, check for any air bubbles that may have surfaced.

6. Release the resin from the mold and finish, if desired. To finish, submerge the resin in a bowl of water, sand with 600-grit sandpaper, polish with 2000-grit sandpaper, and buff with a clean, dry cloth.

finishing

Cured resin has a glossy finish with a waterlike effect, slightly distorting, magnifying, and flattening the images beneath. A satin finish is achieved by using wet and dry sandpapers (600 grit and 2000 grit, respectively, then buff with a cloth to remove any dust or tiny scratches). This effect has a more aged look, and if left unbuffed, will slightly obscure the image beneath with a mistlike, matte quality. The satin technique removes the watery distortion that the glossy surface has and allows light to be dispersed, revealing an undistorted image.

CREATE
THE JEWELRY
OF AN ARTIST
TRAVELING TO
FARAWAY
& MYSTICAL
PLACES

every charm

HAS A

story

Sometimes inspiration is so exquisite, the only explanation for it is magic. This chapter is the home to jewelry projects, each filled with illustrious magic. The chapter begins with a story. A jewelry maker is summoned to create twenty distinct pieces for a group of mysterious friends. With little backstory, the jewelry maker trusts in her client and sets out, traveling to surreal lands and meeting otherworldly creatures. For each piece of jewelry, our traveler enters a portal to other worlds to meet her subjects. While there, she picks up clues to their personalities, sketches patterns and ideas, and notices colors, all of which come into play to create the resulting pieces via easy and unexpected methods.

She documents each of her visits in a sketchbook, which she shares in this chapter, with a diary entry, illustrations, and project notes. Complete materials lists and instructions follow for each entry, many even including a variation on the technique. The result is twenty unique projects and project variations that are utterly personal to the subjects who inspired them. Join this seeker of curiosities. As her story unfolds, so does the magic, and with it, her techniques, materials, tools, and instructions—all of which are of earthly persuasion.

May 15

TODAY WAS ONE OF THE STRANGEST DAYS OF MY LIFE + WOULD PROVE TO BE LESS SO IN DAYS TO COME. I WENT TO MEET A NEW CLIENT, MIRABELLE, WHO'D SEEN MY ARTWORK AT A GALLERY + WANTED TO TALK TO ME ABOUT A COMMISSION. HER MANSION WAS DEEP IN THE COUNTRY AMONGST ROLLING HILLS + FIELDS CARPETED IN WILDFLOWERS. A BEAUTIFUL WOMAN IN CHARCOAL- AND SMOKE-COLORED COUTURE ANSWERED THE ORNATE DOOR, ALL SMILES + WELCOMING.

"THANK YOU FOR COMING! I HOPE YOU FOUND US EASILY ENOUGH?" MIRABELLE ASKED IN A LILTING VOICE. I WONDERED WHO "US" REFERRED TO.

"THANKS. I DIDN'T HAVE ANY PROBLEMS," I SAID, FEELING DOWDY + CLUMSY, WHILE I FOLLOWED HER THROUGH A HOUSE THAT PROBABLY ENTERTAINED ROYALTY.

"THAT'S REASSURING," SHE SMILED. "WOULDN'T WANT YOU WANDERING THROUGH THE WILD WOOD."

"THAT'S A FACT," I SAID, THEN, DECIDING TO GET DOWN TO BUSINESS, "SO, WHAT CAN I DO FOR YOU, MIRABELLE?"

"AH. I NEED YOU TO CRE-ATE JEWELRY FOR MY . . . FRIENDS." THE WAY SHE PAUSED AT "FRIENDS" PIQUED MY CURIOSITY. SHE PROBABLY MEANT BUSINESS ASSOCI-ATES.

"OKAY, THAT SOUNDS GOOD. HOW MANY FOLKS? AND, CASUAL, OR FORMAL?"

"FOR NINETEEN WOMEN, + IT COULD BE EITHER."

"SHOULD THEY ALL MATCH, OR DO YOU WANT THEM ALL DIFFERENT?" I ASKED,

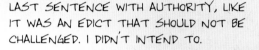

JOTTING DOWN NOTES IN MY SKETCH-
BOOK.

"WHY WOULD I WANT THEM ALL THE
SAME? OH NO, THEY MUST BE
SUITED TO EACH PERSON,
REFLECTING HER, BUT IN YOUR
OWN LOVELY STYLE, OF COURSE."
SHE LOOKED AT ME WITH EYES THE
COLOR OF FADED VIOLETS, SMILING AS IF
I WERE A SILLY CHILD.

"THAT WON'T BE A PROBLEM. COULD YOU
GIVE ME PICTURES + MAYBE TELL ME
A LITTLE ABOUT EACH OF THEM, LIKE
COLORS + THINGS THEY . . ."

"MY DEAR, YOU'LL HAVE TO
MEET WITH THEM!" MIRABELLE IN-
TERRUPTED. "THERE'S SIMPLY NO WAY
I COULD CAPTURE THEIR PERSONALITIES
WITH PHOTOGRAPHS + LISTS!" THEN
SHE ADDED, AFTER SEEING MY FACE, "I
WILL COMPENSATE YOU FOR YOUR TIME,
+ I'LL SEND AN ESCORT WITH YOU, SO
YOU WON'T FEEL AWKWARD." MAYBE SHE
COULD TELL I WAS HORRENDOUSLY SHY,
OR MAYBE SHE COULD SEE THE PANIC I
TRIED TO HIDE.

"ALL RIGHT." I SAID, MY VOICE SMALL,
ALMOST INAUDIBLE. SHE PULLED OUT A
LEATHER ENVELOPE + PASSED IT TO
ME ACROSS AN EBONY COFFEE TABLE.
IT WAS FILLED WITH A GENEROUS
STACK OF BILLS. I SWALLOWED + NODDED.

"THIS SHOULD COVER TRAVEL, YOUR
TIME, + MATERIALS . . . USE
ANYTHING YOU LIKE, BUT THE
PIECES MUST PLEASE MY
FRIENDS. AND I WILL NEED THEM
BY JUNE 24." SHE SAID THIS

LAST SENTENCE WITH AUTHORITY, LIKE
IT WAS AN EDICT THAT SHOULD NOT BE
CHALLENGED. I DIDN'T INTEND TO.

"YOU WON'T BE DISAPPOINTED. I'LL
HAVE EVERYTHING READY BEFORE
THEN."

"THEN WE SHALL DRINK
TO IT, TO SEAL OUR
AGREEMENT!" AT THIS,
SHE BROUGHT OUT A SMALL
GLASS BOTTLE, ROUNDED
+ FROSTED, LIKE IT HAD
TUMBLED IN THE SEA.
SHE POURED DEEP GOLD LIQUID INTO
MATCHING CUPS SMALL ENOUGH FOR
RABBITS TO SIP FROM + PASSED A
CUP TO ME. WE CLINKED CUPS +
I WATCHED HER DOWN HERS IN ONE
GULP. I FOLLOWED SUIT, NOT WANT-
ING TO OFFEND. IT WAS
SWEET + STRONG AND TASTED
WILD + UTTERLY EXOTIC.

"DELICIOUS, ISN'T IT? IT'S MADE
FROM ELDERBERRIES," SHE SAID, SMIL-
ING DREAMILY.

"I'VE NEVER TASTED ANYTHING LIKE IT,"
I SAID + WITH THAT, I STOOD. WE TALKED
AS I HEADED TO THE DOOR.

ON THE WAY HOME, I FELT GIDDY + TERRI-
FIED. I COULDN'T STOP SMILING. THE DRIVE
HOME FELT LIKE A DISTANT MEMORY AS
I WALKED THROUGH MY FRONT GARDEN.
I SAW A FLICKER OF MOVEMENT ON THE
GROUND + PEERED BENEATH THE HOS-
TAS. THE LIGHT MUST HAVE TRICKED
MY EYES, BECAUSE FOR A MOMENT I
THOUGHT I SAW A PROCESSION OF TINY
WINGED PEOPLE, RIDING BIRDS +
FROGS, DRESSED IN MINIATURE FINERY
OF ROSE PETALS
+ DANDELION TUFTS.

studded stones
BRACELET

May 16

EXPECTED A MORE TRADITIONAL METHOD OF COMMUNICATION, NOT THE RED SQUIRREL PECKING AT MY WINDOW WITH A PIECE OF PAPER STICKING OUT OF AN ACORN. THE SQUIRREL LOOKED AT ME, AS IF TO MAKE SURE I SAW + THEN LEAPED TO A TREE BRANCH. I STOOD THERE IN DISBELIEF. I GRABBED THE ACORN & A PIECE OF ACCORDION-FOLDED PARCHMENT SLIPPED OUT.

"SEE YOU AT THREE . . . TOM - YOUR ESCORT," IT SAID.

A TRAINED SQUIRREL? I COULDN'T WAIT TO MEET THIS GUY.

HE ARRIVED EXACTLY AT THREE, BOWING SLIGHTLY WHEN I OPENED THE DOOR. HE CARRIED A GUITAR ON HIS BACK AND A DARK BOX WITH CONTROLS UNDER AN ARM. I NOTICED HE LOOKED STRONG AND VERY HANDSOME. I RESPONDED BY TRIPPING ON MY OWN FEET AND STUTTERING NERVOUSLY ABOUT THE WEATHER. THANKFULLY, HE DIDN'T SEEM TO NOTICE. THEN HE ASKED IN A DEEP VOICE WITH A VERY SLIGHT SCOTTISH ACCENT, "READY TO GO?" HE BEGAN TO FIDDLE WITH THE BOX.

"SURE. WHERE TO?"

"EPHESUS, CITY OF THE AMAZONS . . . WELL, WHERE IT USED TO BE. I GUESS IT'S CALLED TURKEY TODAY," HE SAID IN A MATTER-OF-FACT TONE.

"YEAH, LET ME GET MY JET. IT'S PARKED OUT BACK," I SAID AIRILY. HE PLACED THE BOX ON THE FLOOR + OPENED THE LID. IT WAS LIKE HE OPENED A DOOR OVER THE BOX, AND A RECTANGLE OF BLUE SKY + ROCKY CLIFFS OVER A COBALT BLUE SEA APPEARED. HE STEPPED IN + HELD HIS HAND OUT TO ME, LOOKING AT ME EXPECTANTLY. MAYBE I WAS HALLUCINATING.

WHAT THE HECK. I STEPPED THROUGH, FEELING MOMENTARILY SQUEEZED. I LOOKED BEHIND ME TO SEE MY LIVING ROOM, LOOKING DARK COMPARED TO THE BRILLIANT BLUE OF THE SKY HERE. IN WHAT WAS ONCE EPHESUS. WE WALKED AROUND THE GRASSY CLIFF TOP + WATCHED A WOMAN APPROACH FROM NEAR THE BEACH.

"GREETINGS, FRIENDS," SHE SAID IN A THICK ACCENT. HER HEAVY LIDDED EYES APPRAISED US, SHOWING NO EMOTION. I TOOK IN HER DUST-COLORED DRESS + THE BLUE BELT AROUND HER HIPS + HOW HER HAIR WAS ARRANGED IN ELABORATE BRAIDS.

SHE LED US HIGHER UP, TO WHERE A JUMBLE OF BOULDERS LAY HEAPED. WE STOPPED + SAT, ME NERVOUSLY ARRANGING MY PENCILS + SKETCHBOOK WHILE TOM PLAYED AN ELABORATE SONG ON HIS GUITAR. I ASKED HER WHAT SHE WOULD LIKE + SHE SHRUGGED, AMBIVALENT.

"MAKE ME SOMETHING I'LL LIKE."

OKAY. SHE SMILED THEN + IT WAS LIKE HER FACE CAME ALIVE. I HOPED THAT WHATEVER I MADE WOULD CHEER HER. I NOTED THE LANDSCAPE WITH A DRAWING, THE PATTERN ON HER DRESS WITH WATER-COLORED WAVES. I WOULD USE THE COLORS OF BOULDERS, OF DEEP OCEAN WATER, MAYBE THE RED OF THE STONES AT HER FEET.

studded stones
BRACELET

⟶ Polymer beads studded with nail heads are reminiscent of stones and old gold. These earthy baubles could have been worn by those from ancient civilizations long fallen. The polymer beads are given character by their wood-grain texture and sparkly inclusions of foil. Use as many or as few nail heads as you like to stud your polymer clay beads. The nail heads will reflect light, creating points of interest. ⟶

BEAD MATERIALS

Polymer clay

24 brass 1" (2.5 cm) finishing nails

CLAY COLOR FORMULAS

Deep blue 1 part teal, 1 part navy, 2 parts pearlescent blue, 1 part pearlescent bronze, 1 pinch foil

Crimson 1 part dark red, 1 part pearlescent red, 1 part dark brown, 1 pinch foil

TOOLS

Polymer clay toolbox (page 20)

Mandrel

Flush cutters

Polishing cloth

FINISHED SIZE

7" (18 cm)

STUDDED POLYMER BEADS

1⟶ Condition the polymer clay before mixing the clay color formulas (for more details on faux wood texture, see page 24). Mix enough to create 4 crimson beads and 1 deep blue.

2⟶ Roll balls into the desired size of bead (these are between ¾" [1.9cm] and 1" [2.5cm]).

3⟶ Pierce the polymer clay balls with a mandrel, adjust the shape, and place in the freezer for 15 minutes to harden the clay.

4⟶ Cut the finishing nail heads with flush cutters to ¼" (6 mm).

5⟶ Press the trimmed nails into the beads, being careful not to distort the shape.

6⟶ Bake. Finish as desired (these are polished with a cloth).

BRACELET MATERIALS

11 mocha 4mm Swarovski crystal bicones

12 Caribbean blue 4mm Swarovski crystal bicones

12 satin peach 4mm Swarovski crystal bicones

24 golden shadow 4mm Swarovski crystal sequins

2 raku 6mm rounds

5 agate 13x10mm irregular drilled pebbles

4 crimson ¾" (1.9cm) studded polymer clay rounds

1 deep blue 1" (2.5cm) studded polymer clay round

3" (7.6 cm) of oxidized silver 24-gauge wire

1 oxidized silver 13x9mm lobster clasp

6" (15 cm) of gold-tone 4x6mm chain

46 fine silver drawn 1½" (3.8 cm) head pins

TOOLS

Wire toolbox (page 16)

BRACELET INSTRUCTIONS

1~ Using 3" (7.6 cm) of the 24-gauge wire, fancy wrap the lobster clasp to the 6" (15 cm) piece of 4x6mm cable chain.

2~ Use 3 balled head pins to create 3 wire-wrapped dangles (see page 17), each strung with three 4mm bicones (in this pattern: mocha, blue, peach) onto the chain.

3~ Stack a golden shadow 4mm crystal sequin, 1 raku 6mm round, and a 4mm crystal sequin onto a head pin and attach to the chain. Repeat Step 2.

4~ Stack a golden shadow 4mm crystal sequin, an agate pebble, and a 4mm crystal sequin onto a head pin and attach to the chain, following the three crystals. Wire wrap 3 crystal dangles in the same pattern. Then stack a golden shadow 4mm crystal sequin, a crimson polymer clay bead, and a 4mm crystal sequin onto a head pin, and then attach to the chain.

5~ Repeat this pattern four times, placing the large 1" (2.5cm) blue polymer bead in the middle. Repeat Step 2.

6~ Stack 1 golden shadow 4mm crystal sequin, 1 raku 6mm round, and one 4mm crystal sequin onto a head pin and attach to the chain.

✳VARIATION

The same bead technique was used to create this matching necklace.

antonia's
PENDANT

May 18

THE WONDROUS JOURNEY OF THE DAY BEFORE LEFT ME FEELING LIKE THE BEARER OF AN INCREDIBLE SECRET, ONE THAT I COULDN'T POSSIBLY SHARE. I FELT DAZZLED THAT I LIVED IN A WORLD WITH SUCH MAGIC.

THE NEXT MESSAGE WAS DELIVERED COURTESY OF A HOUSE SPARROW. THE NOTE READ, "TODAY AT NOON-TOM." I HAD A COUPLE OF HOURS, SO I MADE PISTACHIO SHORTBREAD COOKIES + PACKED A DAY BAG.

HE KNOCKED AT NOON + WE STARTED WITH LITTLE CONVERSATION. I FELT SHY AROUND HIM + DIDN'T WANT TO EXHIBIT MY CLUMSINESS WHEN I SPOKE. THE ONLY THING HE SAID WAS,

"TODAY WE ARE GOING TO VENICE, NEAR SAN MARCO."

I WAS ELATED, HAVING HARBORED A DESIRE TO VISIT THE CITY EVER SINCE I'D SEEN A PICTURE. WHEN HE OPENED THE DOOR, THE VIEW OVERLOOKED TILED ROOFTOPS + A GOLDEN DOME. I STEPPED THROUGH + FOUND MYSELF ON A HIGH VERANDA. I STEPPED TO THE EDGE + SAW THE CITY SPREAD OUT BELOW-THE CANALS, WEAVING THROUGH BUILDINGS LABYRINTHINE AND NARROW. MY BREATH CAUGHT WHEN I STUDIED THE DOMES OF SAN MARCO-MORE BEAUTIFUL THAN I IMAGINED.

THE FEELING OF ADMIRATION WAS REPLACED WITH AMAZEMENT AS A DARK SHAPE FLEW TOWARD US, GRADUALLY BECOMING . . .

AN ANGEL. SUCH A TERM DIDN'T QUITE CAPTURE THE BEING WHO LANDED GRACEFULLY ON THE LEDGE, SILHOUETTED AGAINST THE TWILIGHT. BIRD QUALITIES HUNG AROUND HER, RATHER THAN THOSE OF THE DIVINE. HER HAIR SHONE BLUE-BLACK AGAINST WHITE SKIN THAT CONTRASTED WITH HER DARK GOWN. HER WINGS WERE SPOTTED + IRIDESCENT LIKE A STARLING'S IN WINTER. WE INTRODUCED OURSELVES, + SHE TOLD US HER NAME, ANTONIA, IN A HUSKY ITALIAN ACCENT.

"SO . . . HOW LONG HAVE YOU LIVED IN VENICE?" I ASKED MILDLY, TRYING NOT TO STARE AT HER VELVETY WINGS.

"I CAME HERE AROUND 1497, WHEN I LEFT FLORENCE," SHE SAID, LOOKING OUT OVER THE CITY, HER VOICE DISTANT WITH RECOLLECTION. "THE WORLD HAD CHANGED SO MUCH! MY FLORENCE WAS ONCE THE CENTER OF EVERYTHING! PAINTING + LITERATURE, IT WAS A GOLDEN AGE, THE RENAISSANCE!" SHE TURNED AS SHE SPOKE, HER EYES ALIGHT WITH PRIDE + IN THAT MOMENT I SAW THE MUSE OF PAINTERS, SCULPTORS + POETS. HAD I SEEN HER IMAGE IN A BOTTICELLI?

WE TALKED WELL INTO THE NIGHT + IT WAS ALMOST MORNING WHEN WE RETURNED TO MY HOUSE. I KNEW THAT I HAD TO CAPTURE HER LOVE OF DECADENCE, OF PERFECT FORMS + OPULENCE, AS I TAPED A FEW DARK, SPECKLED FEATHERS THAT HAD FALLEN INTO MY BOOK.

antonia's PENDANT

❧ Luminous polymer eggs decorated with vintage glass gems and crystal flat backs are reminiscent of sunlit domes and Fabergé eggs. These simple pendants are fast to make and easy to alter. For a more rustic look, try using pieces of sea glass, bits of mirror, or tumbled stones to embed in the pendants. ❧

PENDANT MATERIALS

Polymer clay

5 clear crystal 8x12mm foiled teardrop flat-back rhinestones

5 ruby ABx2 ss16 Swarovski foiled Xilion Rose flat-back rhinestones

10 Indian pink ss8 Swarovski foiled Xilion Rose flat-back rhinestones

Two-part epoxy adhesive

CLAY COLOR FORMULA

1 part copper, ½ part red sparkle, ¼ part bronze sparkle, 1 pinch foil

TOOLS

Polymer clay toolbox (page 20)

Mandrel

Wooden tool

Sandpaper (500 , 700 , 1000 , 2000 grits)

Polishing cloth

FINISHED SIZE

16½" (42 cm)

EGG PENDANT

1~ Condition the polymer clay before mixing the clay color formula.

2~ Roll the polymer clay into 1 egg shape.

3~ Pierce with a mandrel. Refrigerate.

4~ Press crystal flat backs into the surface, maintaining the shape. Bake according to the manufacturer's instructions.

5~ Remove the crystals with a wooden tool by gently prying up after baking and then polish. To polish, lightly wet sand with a piece of 500-grit sandpaper, 700-grit sandpaper, 1000-grit sandpaper, and then 2000-grit sandpaper. Do not oversand. If you sand too much, your rhinestone indentations will be lost. Buff lightly with a polishing cloth.

6~ Glue the crystals back into place with a two-part epoxy adhesive. Do not use Super Glue, it will create a foggy residue on the crystal surfaces.

*note TRY INCORPORATING THE NAIL-HEAD-STUDDED POLYMER CLAY TECHNIQUE FROM THE PREVIOUS PROJECT WITH VARYING SIZES, SHAPES, + COLORS OF CRYSTAL FLAT-BACK RHINESTONES IN UNIQUE PATTERNS TO CREATE PERSONALIZED EMBELLISHED EGG PENDANTS.

58

NECKLACE MATERIALS

1 topaz 4×7mm cubic zirconia drop

1 polymer clay egg pendant

30 Thai silver 2mm cornerless cubes

6 golden shadow 4mm Swarovski crystal bicones

10 satin padparadscha 4mm Swarovski crystal bicones

6 copper crystal 4mm Swarovski crystal bicones

6 golden shadow 6mm Swarovski crystal bicones

14 golden shadow 5mm Swarovski crystal-encrusted rondelles

4 golden shadow 12×8mm Swarovski crystal polygons

40 sunstone 5mm rondelles

2 golden shadow 12×10mm Swarovski crystal cosmic cut beads

12" (30 cm) of gold-filled 22-gauge wire

18" (46 cm) of bronze .019 flexible beading wire

2 gold-filled 2×2mm crimp tubes

1 shibuichi bird toggle clasp

TOOLS

Wire toolbox (page 16)

NECKLACE INSTRUCTIONS

1— Using 4" (10 cm) of the 22-gauge gold-filled wire and 1 faceted CZ drop, form a fancy-wrapped wire dangle. Using 8" (20 cm) of the 22-gauge gold-filled wire, form a fancy-wrapped link. Form a wire-wrapped loop (see page 17). String 1 embellished polymer clay egg. Attach the wire-wrapped dangle to the bottom loop. Set aside.

2— Cut 18" (46 cm) of bronze .019 flexible beading wire. String 1 crimp tube. Attach to half of the toggle clasp.

3— String 1 cornerless cube, 1 golden shadow 4mm bicone, 1 cornerless cube, 1 padparadscha 4mm bicone, 1 cornerless cube, 1 copper crystal 4mm bicone, 1 cornerless cube, 1 padparadscha 4mm bicone, 1 cornerless cube, 1 golden shadow 4mm bicone, 1 cornerless cube, 1 padparadscha 4mm bicone, 1 cornerless cube, 1 copper crystal 4mm bicone, 1 cornerless cube, 1 padparadscha 4mm bicone, 1 golden shadow 4mm bicone, 1 cornerless cube, 1 copper crystal 4mm bicone, 1 cornerless cube, 1 golden shadow 6mm bicone, 1 cornerless cube, 1 golden shadow 6mm bicone, 1 cornerless cube, 1 golden shadow 6mm bicone, 1 golden shadow 5mm crystal-encrusted rondelle, 5 sunstone 5mm rondelles, 1 golden shadow 5mm crystal-encrusted rondelle, 1 golden shadow 12×8 crystal polygon, 1 golden shadow 5mm crystal-encrusted rondelle, 5 sunstone 5mm rondelles, 1 golden shadow 12×8 crystal polygon, 1 golden shadow 5mm crystal encrusted rondelle, 5 sunstone 5mm rondelles, 1 golden shadow 5mm crystal-encrusted rondelle, 1 golden shadow 12mm crystal cosmic bead, 1 golden shadow 5mm crystal encrusted rondelle, 4 sunstone 5mm rondelles, 1 cornerless cube, 1 padparadscha 4mm bicone, and 1 cornerless cube.

4— String the embellished polymer clay egg pendant from Step 1. Repeat the sequence from Step 3 in reverse to complete the other half. String 1 crimp tube. Attach to the remaining half of the toggle.

*VARIATION

These earrings use the same technique, only simplified.

petal
cascade

May 20

A note dropped from the beak of a crow. It read, "Tonight at 6-Tom."
   I wondered if he trained the animals or if they just did his bidding, like some kind of critter master. My door opened to a surly Tom at five minutes past six. I wanted to ask what was going on, but thought better of it.

"So, where are we going today, Tom?"

"If you give me a moment, I'll inform you," he said a little icier than necessary.

"All right, you just take your time. I'll wait until it's convenient for you." There was no masking the sarcasm or the hurt beneath my words. He said nothing for a while, watching me pack my bag with my art supplies, vanilla cupcakes + strawberry vanilla tea in a thermos. He sighed deeply + spoke softly.

"I'm sorry. My day has been unpleasant. We are going to a very remote location in Japan."

"Fine." {I could've let it go, but I didn't.}

We stepped out of my living room into a beautiful, neatly kept garden at the base of an immense mountain. I saw an ancient temple in the shadow of black pines, the stones once a burnished gold, now faded to a dull beige. I could see a woman in a kimono approach.

She was TINY, HER HAIR, PALE AS CLOUDS, swirled around her head like it was underwater. She said her name was Mae. We sat beneath a sakura tree, overlooking a pond with black swans + a miniature island in the middle. I let Mae serve the tea + cupcakes.

I noticed then how otherworldly she seemed, her spider silk kimono shining, her skin glowing lightly. I considered HOW PALE STONES WOULD LOOK ON HER SKIN + thought I'd use leaf shapes + something that tinkled when she moved. Our meeting didn't last long, + we were in my living room scarcely an hour later. I wondered aloud what kind of being she was, + Tom answered.

"When she was much younger, her uncle caught + killed a mermaid, for food." He paused to allow me to absorb the shocking information.

"He prepared a little of it to try + gave some to Mae. He died instantly, because it's poisonous to males. Mae, on the other hand, will never die. She will remain young forever + possesses a little magical ability."

"So, she ate mermaid meat + now she's immortal?" I wondered whether that was why her coloring looked strange. I wondered what mermaid tasted like. I began to giggle.

"YEAH," he smiled a genuine, slightly lopsided grin + I wasn't mad anymore.

petal cascade

A geisha's hairpin and earrings made from polished polymer, shrink film, silver, and sparkling crystals jingle soothingly with movement. Charms made from shrink-plastic film are easy to create and decorate. Their light weight also makes them perfect for clustering in large, dahlia-like shapes. Some shrink-plastic film can be run through a home printer. Use this option to create uniform multiples or to incorporate your favorite design without having to freehand draw it.

CHARM MATERIALS

Plastic shrink film

TOOLS

Sandpaper (300 to 400 grit)
Scissors
Corner-rounder tool (optional)
Hole punch
Permanent markers or colored pencils
Metal pan
Parchment paper
Spatula

FINISHED SIZES

8¼" (21 cm) total—6" (15 cm) hair-stick, 2¼" (6 cm) dangle

PLASTIC SHRINK PETALS

1— Prepare the plastic shrink film by sanding the entire sheet in one direction and then in the other with 300- to 400-grit sandpaper (this is easier than sanding small pieces, one at a time). Sanding allows the ink to grab the surface.

2— Cut out three petal shapes three times larger than desired with sturdy scissors (shrink film can shrink anywhere from 50 to 70 percent of the original size). Round any sharp corners (or use a corner-rounder tool) and use a hole punch to create holes.

3— Using permanent markers or colored pencils, draw designs on the sanded plastic shrink film. Test permanence by wetting slightly and touching the surface. If it smears, use another marker.

4— Bake according to the manufacturer's instructions (line metal pans with a sheet of parchment to prevent the plastic from sticking). If you are having trouble getting the petals perfectly flat, try pressing them gently with a flexible spatula while the plastic shrink film is still hot, pulled straight out of the oven.

HAIRPIN MATERIALS

Metal clay

Slip

Polymer clay (1 part each navy, dark blue pearl, teal)

3 shrink-plastic 27×11mm petals

3 labradorite 3×7mm drops

3 silver 8×14mm petal-shaped sequins

1" (2.5 cm) of silver 4mm round cable chain

4 silver 6mm jump rings

3 silver 4mm jump rings

5½" (14 cm) of silver 24-gauge wire

TOOLS

Wire toobox (page 16)

Metal clay toolbox (page 25)

Polymer clay toolbox (page 20)

Craft knife

Dowel

Pencil

Straw

Wooden cuticle stick

Sandpaper (400 to 2000 grit)

HAIRPIN INSTRUCTIONS

1— Roll out a thin sheet of metal clay and cut out a strip about ⅝" wide × 1" high (1.6 × 2.5 cm).

2— Wrap the strip around a dowel and smooth the seam. Allow the metal clay tube to dry.

3— Roll out a thin sheet of metal clay and use a pencil to trace around the bottom edge of the metal clay tube to make a cap of metal clay. Attach with slip and let dry.

4— Use the bottom edge of the tube and a craft knife to measure out another circle. Remove the center of the circle by punching it with a straw. Slice the ring in half and let it dry. Attach the loop to the top of the cap with slip.

5— Fire and finish the cap.

6— Condition three ¾" (10 cm) balls of polymer clay in navy, dark blue pearl, and teal. Mix all the colors.

7— Trim a wooden cuticle stick to 5½" (14 cm) and cover the stick with the polymer clay. Roll the polymer clay into a log and push the stick into it, to avoid trapping air. Smooth out the polymer clay, gently rolling it into shape, not too vigorously or it will peel away from the stick. Using a straw, press small holes in the surface of the polymer clay and fill in later.

8— Insert the raw polymer clay–covered cuticle stick into the finished metal clay cap, adjusting the fit.

9— Bake and fill in the depressions left with the straw with a lighter colored polymer clay. Press firmly and smooth the polymer clay evenly into the depressions. Bake again.

10— Sand to reveal the design and polish the surface with a progression of sandpapers, from 400 to 2000 grit, for a glossy look. Be careful not to scratch the metal clay cap.

11— Attach the 1" (2.5 cm) silver round cable chain to the hairpin with 1 silver 6mm jump ring.

12— Equally space the shrink film petals along the chain and attach with 4mm jump rings.

13— Wire wrap 1 labradorite 3×7 drop above each petal on the chain.

14— Using a silver 6mm jump ring, add 1 silver 8×14 petal-shaped sequin on the cap's loop. Then add another on the second and fourth link of the chain.

✳VARIATION

Matching earrings were made to accompany the hairpin.

owl ojime NECKLACE

Pebbleall

May 22

THIS TIME THE MESSAGE GAVE ME TWO DAYS TO PREPARE. I BOUGHT A NEW DRESS + HAD EVERYTHING PACKED IN MY BAG, INCLUDING THE HOT CHOCOLATE + THE BANANA BREAD, WHEN HE ARRIVED PROMPTLY AT FOUR.

"WE ARE HEADED TO A VERY RURAL PART OF TUSCANY, TO SEE A LADY WHO ENJOYS COOKING, I'M TOLD," HE SMILED AT MY EX-PRESSION, WHICH MUST HAVE BEEN RAPT.

"WELL, LET'S GO! I'M READY!"

WE STEPPED INTO WHAT LOOKED LIKE THE BACKGROUND OF A DA VINCI PAINTING: UN-DULATING HILLS, BAY TREES + ROSEMARY BUSHES. I BREATHED DEEPLY WHILE I FOL-LOWED HIM TO A STONE HOUSE. THE WOMAN WHO ANSWERED THE DOOR LOOKED ORDINARY AT FIRST, BUT AS WE SPOKE, HER IMAGE BLURRED + I COULD SEE HER HOOVED FEET + THE SPIRALING HORNS NESTLED IN HER THICK RED CURLS. IN A FADED BROGUE SHE SAID HER NAME WAS LAYLA + LED US INTO HER KITCHEN. IT SMELLED LIKE HEAVEN. BREAD ROLLS EMERGED FROM THE OVEN, CRUSTY + FRAGRANT, WHILE LOBSTER SIM-MERED IN BUTTER + GARLIC. SHE ASKED US TO SET THE TABLE + WE JUMPED INTO EFFICIENCY. WE DINED ON COLORFUL PLATES TOPPED WITH SALAD + PASTA HEAPED HIGH WITH THE BUTTERY LOBSTER. I NEARLY MOANED IN ABSOLUTE HAPPINESS.

WE LINGERED AT THE TABLE FOR A LONG TIME + SHE TOLD US STORIES OF HER YOUTH, ABOUT BEING WILD IN HER MOTHER'S COUNTRY + THE DANGERS OF DRAGONS.

I BROUGHT OUT MY BANANA BREAD + HOT CHOCOLATE + SHE PRAISED ME UNTIL MY FACE BURNED WITH PLEASURE. I WAS SURPRISED TO NOTICE TWO OWLS ROOSTING IN THE RAFTERS OF THE HIGH CEILING, HOOTING TO ONE ANOTHER. SHE NOTICED ME LOOKING + SAID, AMIABLY, "AH, YOU SEE MY LOVELY DARLINGS! THEY ARE MY HAP-PINESS, THOSE TWO!"

"THEY ARE SO BEAUTIFUL!"

I SAID SIMPLY, THEN ASKED HESITANTLY, "ARE THEY MAGICAL?"

"WHY, YES! THEY CAN MAKE HUMAN FACES, IF THEY WANT TO TALK TO ME," SHE SAID. "HEY, SALLY! JOE! LET'S SHOW OUR NEW FRIENDS YOUR FACES."

THE OWLS SHIVERED, DUCKED THEIR HEADS UNDER A WING + THEN PULLED THEM OUT, SHOWING CHILDLIKE FACES, SMILING DOWN AT US. WE CLAPPED FOR THEM + THEY BEGAN TO SING BAWDY SONGS, FIT FOR SAILORS. WE LAUGHED UNTIL OUR SIDES HURT, THEY WERE SO GOOD. THEN TOM PLAYED ALONG WITH THEM, STRUM-MING HIS GUITAR + SINGING.

I WATCHED LAYLA, HOW HER MANY LAYERED SKIRTS SWIRLED AROUND HER IN DEEP BLUES + COPPERS. I WANTED TO CAPTURE WHAT SHE LOVED, HER OWLS + THE COLORS OF HER HOMELAND.

"LET'S OPEN A BOTTLE OF MY NEIGHBOR'S BREW," LAYLA SAID. SHE WAS ALREADY UNCORK-ING A BOTTLE BEFORE I COULD ANSWER.

"I SUPPOSE IT COULDN'T HURT . . ." I SAID.

JOE

SALLY

65

owl ojime NECKLACE

This sweet owl was created in the style of antique Japanese *ojime* beads (decorative pieces used to closed lidded boxes that hung from kimono belts). The owl bead was sculpted from polymer clay. Various colors of polymer were layered to create the look of faux ivory and faux wood.

PENDANT MATERIALS
Polymer clay

2 carnelian ss12 cabochons

Burnt umber acrylic paint

CLAY COLOR FORMULA
1 part cream, 1 part tan, 2 parts translucent, 1 part white (see page 24 for more details on creating faux ivory)

TOOLS
Polymer clay toolbox (page 20)

Mandrel

Paintbrush

FINISHED SIZE
21" (53 cm)

FAUX IVORY OWL PENDANT

1— Form faux ivory polymer clay into a flattened egg shape and pierce it with a mandrel. Build the owl with two flat teardrops for wings and a heart shape for the face. Press the cabochons into the heart shape for the eyes.

2— Shape a small teardrop of clay for the beak. Using a wooden tool with a flat edge, inscribe feather details around eyes and on wings and belly.

3— Fire according to the manufacturer's instructions and finish as desired. Once cool, coat with a wash of burnt umber acrylic paint to enhance details and create an aged-ivory effect.

NECKLACE MATERIALS

36 vermeil 3mm cornerless cubes

13 faceted 6mm carnelian rounds

1 sterling silver 4mm Thai eye bead

4 vermeil 10mm Thai flat rounds

3 faceted 9mm sleeping beauty turquoise rounds

1 owl pendant

2 gold 5×10mm paddles

1 ruby 6×8mm cubic zirconia

16½" (42 cm) of sterling silver 20-gauge wire

1 sterling silver bird toggle clasp

3½" (9 cm) of sterling silver 4×6mm cable chain

3 silver 5mm jump rings

TOOLS

Wire toolbox (page 16)

NECKLACE INSTRUCTIONS

1~ Using 2" (5 cm) of wire, form a simple loop. Attach to half of the toggle clasp. String 1 vermeil 3mm cornerless cube, 1 faceted 6mm carnelian round, and 1 vermeil 3mm cornerless cube. Form another simple loop. Repeat twelve times. Attach each link to the previous loop to create a wire-wrapped link chain. Set aside.

2~ Using 1½" (4 cm) of wire, form a simple loop. Attach to the remaining half of the toggle clasp. String 1 vermeil 3mm cornerless cube, 1 sterling silver 4mm Thai eye bead, and 1 vermeil 3mm cornerless cube. Form another simple loop. Attach to the end of a 1³/₈" (4 cm) length of chain.

3~ Using 2" (5 cm) of wire, form a simple loop. Attach to the last link of the chain. String 1 vermeil 10mm Thai flat round. Form a simple loop. Attach to a ½" (2 cm) length of chain. Using 2½" (7 cm) of wire, form a simple loop. Attach to the last link of the chain. String 1 vermeil 3mm cornerless cube, 1 faceted 9mm turquoise round, and 1 vermeil 3mm cornerless cube. Form a simple loop. Attach to a ½" (2 cm) length of chain.

4~ Repeat Step 3 twice. Connect to the previous lengths. Using 1½" (4 cm) of wire, form a simple loop. Attach to the last link of the chain. String 1 vermeil 10mm Thai flat round. Close with a simple loop.

5~ Using 3" (8 cm) of wire, form a simple loop. Attach the ends of both halves of the necklace. String the ivory owl ojime bead. Form a simple loop.

6~ Open 1 silver 5mm jump ring. String 1 vermeil 3mm cornerless cube and 1 gold 5×10 paddle. Close the jump ring. Attach the loop from the previous step and a ½" (2 cm) length of chain. Open 1 silver 5mm jump ring and string 1 gold 5×10 paddle. Close the jump ring. Attach to the first link of the chain. Open 1 silver 5mm jump ring. Add 1 vermeil 3mm cornerless cube and 1 ruby CZ. Close the ring on the last link of chain.

✱ VARIATION

You can use the same process to make faux wood, just alter the colors to pale golds and tans for light wood and deep sienna and dark umber for mahogany.

sculptural
scrimshaw
COLLAR

May 23

Layla's neighbor made an excellent wine, the evidence of which was thumping through my skull. I ignored the pale gold cat meowing at my window, a small red pouch on the sill. Maybe it would go away. It didn't. I finally got up to look at the note, then at the clock. I had about twenty minutes before Tom arrived. I hurled myself into the shower, then threw on jeans + a t-shirt just as the door knocker announced Tom's arrival. He stared at my wet hair streaming around my shoulders, + I took in his hollow eyes. We smirked at each other sheepishly, as he went directly to the coffee pot.

"Allow me," he said, making up a pot. I sat down on the couch + waited. He brought me a cup after rummaging through my messy cabinets.

"Today we will venture into the desert between UTAH + COLORADO," he said quietly, sipping his own coffee.

"Oh, good. Scorching heat + dehydration," I said, then added, "better bring some water."

We emerged from the cavernous dark of my living room into blinding light. When my eyes adjusted, I could see a treacherous landscape, not exactly desert, with the SCRUBBY PINES standing in groups. From where we stood, we could see what looked like a city carved out of the side of the cliff wall.

SPIRALING PATTERN

"What is that place?" I asked.

"It's called Mesa Verde. It used to be an amazing community of the Anasazi. They abandoned it five hundred years ago when a drought or war drove them away + now most of it has collapsed."

We made our way down to the bottom of the cliff, picking through the THORNY BUSHES + walking along a steep path. When we reached the ancient dwellings, I felt as though someone was watching us, so we waited. Eventually, a strange creature crept from a cave, moving slowly + looking like she wanted to run. I felt the same way as I took in the lovely face atop A SPOTTED DEER body. She looked small against the entry, her head reaching my waist. She seemed wild, her GOLDEN EYES alarmed.

"Hi!" I said, feeling silly. She almost ran. I was tired + in pain, so I sat on a boulder + waited. Tom joined me in silence + then she approached. I told her our names + she whispered, "NIABI." I drew a picture of her, attempting to capture her grace + lithe form. I sketched the SPIRALING PATTERN ON HER COAT, NOTING THE WAY IT RESEMBLED IVORY INLAID IN WOOD. She watched us for a while, never coming close, never speaking. We returned to my house, + I felt sad for the deer girl + wondered what her smile looked like.

69

sculptural scrimshaw
COLLAR

⟶ Derived from a sailors' technique of engraving whale bone and rubbing ink into the lines, this method of carving out designs and filling with clay echoes the older tradition. This method is quite addictive, as sanding and polishing the surface reveals the pattern crisply, which grows more luminous as it's polished. Try using this technique with beads as well as flat pendants. ⟶

**PENDANT
MATERIALS**
Polymer clay

**CLAY COLOR
FORMULA**
1 part teal, 1 part navy, 1 part blue sparkle, ½ part bronze, 1 pinch foil. Each part is ½" (1.3 cm).

TOOLS
Polymer clay toolbox (page 20)
Wooden tool
Pencil and tracing paper (optional)
Straw
Sandpaper (320 to 2000 grit)
Polishing cloth

PENDANT

1 ~ Condition the polymer clay and shape into a crescent ¼" (6 mm) thick.

2 ~ Using a wooden tool, press a design into the clay, or transfer an image first with pencil and tracing paper (see instructions on page 41). Poke holes at each end with a straw. Include holes for dangles.

3 ~ Bake according to the manufacturer's instructions and allow to cool.

4 ~ For a gradated effect, use two or three colors of clay to press into the depressions, blending them well.

5 ~ Bake. Wet sand (320 to 2000 grit) to reveal the design and then polish to a high shine.

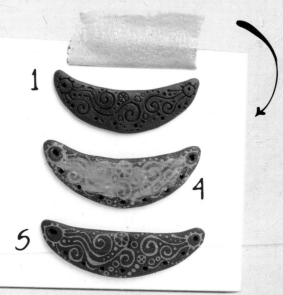

NECKLACE MATERIALS

106 silver 2mm seed beads

2 silver 2mm cornerless cubes

2 kyanite 13×18mm ovals

2 kyanite 14×10mm ovals

60 labradorite 4mm rounds

7 labradorite 10×7mm teardrops

1 polymer clay pendant

4 silver 2×2mm crimp tubes

17" (43 cm) of silver .014 fine flexible beading wire

6 silver 5mm irregular spacers

1 metal clay toggle clasp
(see page 29 for instructions)

10½" (27 cm) of silver 24-gauge wire

TOOLS

Wire toolbox (page 16)

FINISHED SIZE

18" (46 cm)

NECKLACE INSTRUCTIONS

1~ String 1 silver 2×2mm crimp tube and 19 silver 2mm seed beads onto an 8½" (22 cm) length of beading wire. Carefully pass the silver-beaded end of the wire through the first hanging hole at the top of the pendant and back through the crimp tube. Crimp the tube, forming a beaded loop.

2~ String 1 silver cornerless cube, 1 silver 5mm irregular spacer, 1 kyanite 13×18mm oval, 1 silver 5mm irregular spacer, 1 kyanite 14×10mm oval, 1 silver 5mm irregular spacer.

3~ String 1 labradorite 4mm round and 1 silver 2mm seed bead. Repeat the pattern twenty-nine times.

4~ String 4 silver 2mm seed beads and use 1 silver 2×2mm crimp tube to attach one half of the metal clay toggle.

5~ Repeat Steps 1 through 4 for the other side.

6~ Use 1½" (3.8 cm) of silver 24-gauge wire to create a wire-wrapped dangle (see page 17), strung with 1 labradorite 10×7mm teardrop, attaching to the first hole on the bottom edge of the polymer clay pendant. Repeat six times for the remaining holes.

*VARIATION

This pendant features foil inclusions and powders to give the clay a luminous quality. The translucent ivory pattern contrasts against the deep background.

window
of the
heart
BEZEL PENDANT

May 25

When the message dropped from a bluebird, I couldn't help but feel excited. Tom arrived, looking very polished in a white button-down shirt + gray slacks. I excused myself and changed into a pretty dress with a shocking neckline. I called from my room, "Where to today?"

"One of my favorite cities . . . FLORENCE!" I came out + blushed when I saw his reaction, which was quickly disguised as he fumbled with the box.

We left my cozy living room to step into a cobblestone alley, tall buildings flanking either side of us. We walked around the corner to a cafe with outdoor seating + found a table. We ordered ITALIAN HOT CHOCOLATE at Tom's insistence + I felt like I was sipping thick, sweet, liquid happiness.

"BUON GIORNO, I AM CARMINA," said a voice behind us.

She regarded us with a sly expression, + I noted she looked like a fashionable shop girl with MESMERIZING EYES + CROPPED HAIR. She looked at Tom lingeringly + I found myself annoyed, then shook the feeling off. He was just a friend.

We decided to walk around + headed out into the dusk. The city vibrated with activity as we passed food stands, leather shops, bookstores + gelato shops. Carmina smiled amiably, leading us through the bustling streets, commenting on statues I recognized from art history classes. We approached a particularly crowded area, the PONTE VECCHIO BRIDGE + made our way across the river, past the stores + people. I stopped at an amazing MASK SHOP, the window filled with gilt + feathered papier-mache. We went in and tried on a few, laughing at our reflections. The little old woman at the register stared at Carmina, said something in Italian + rushed into the back room. We stared after her + then left.

"WHAT WAS THAT ABOUT?" I asked.

"She was afraid + said she didn't sell to VAMPIRES," answered Carmina.

"OH. ARE YOU A VAMPIRE?" I asked, feeling my face go slack.

"I won't harm you." She smiled + began to tell us her story. "I come from the dark folk, malicious beings, devoid of kindness. I could not live the way they did, always living in the shadows, always moving. I ran away, but they pursued me, outraged. I met Mirabelle + she helped me escape. I've lived here ever since."

She stopped to look at us directly, her eyes wet, then quickly thanked us + left. I stared after her, wondering about her life + something about this evening filled my head with LITTLE RELIQUARIES, the idea of preserving a token forever.

window of the heart
BEZEL PENDANT

➤A lovely polymer heart, with a window carved in the middle, is filled with tiny things. These feature watch crystals and a pretty little bird sculpted from black polymer clay and dry-brushed with metallic gold paint. This piece can also be made by filling the window with resin and adding pieces of wet-media acetate (clear plastic film once used by designers to paint text over pictures without painting on the actual picture; it is available at most art supply stores) to paint decorative images that appear to float within. ➤

PENDANT MATERIALS
Polymer clay

Brass or silver 20-gauge wire

Resin or watch crystal and liquid polymer

Tiny objects

CLAY COLOR FORMULA
1 part crimson, ¼ part red sparkle, ¼ part bronze, 1 pinch foil

TOOLS
Polymer clay toolbox (page 20)

Resin toolbox (page 45)

Wooden tool

Tile

Circle cutter

Sandpaper (300 to 2000 grit)

Buffing cloth

Tape

Soap and warm water

PENDANT

1— Condition the polymer clay, mixing it together with the color and shaping it into a heart.

2— Create a wire-wrapped loop of brass or silver 20-gauge wire, spreading the ends out to hold the clay better. Press into the top of the heart until only the loop shows. Use a wooden tool to clean up around loop.

3— Place the heart on a tile and cut out a shape with a circle cutter, avoiding the loop ends. To make the window frame, roll out a thin sheet of clay and use the circle cutter to cut out a circle border for the window. Press to the heart, around the window, and decorate with wooden tools and glass stones if desired.

4— Bake. Wet sand (300 to 2000 grit) and polish the heart with a soft buffing cloth.

5— Fill the cavity.

5

TO FILL WITH RESIN
Use clear tape to seal the back of the heart. Press firmly so that no resin will leak out. Turn over and fill with objects, painted wet-media acetate, or other items. Pour the resin according to the manufacturer's instructions into the empty cavity. Once set, remove the tape and scrub with warm water and soap to remove any residue left from the sticky tape. Pour multiple layers of resin to add depth between embedded objects. Allow the previous layer to cure before pouring the next.

TO USE A WATCH CRYSTAL

Roll out a sheet of polymer clay. Cut out a frame from the polymer clay sheet that is the same diameter as the shape that was cut into the heart. Place the crystal over the opening on the heart. Apply a thin coat of liquid polymer to the back of the frame and gently place the frame on top of the heart to secure the crystal in place. Bake. Fill with objects and repeat the window steps for the other side.

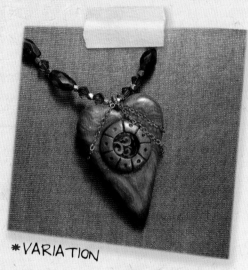

*VARIATION

The bezel can be filled with resin or small objects. Tiny objects are lightly contained by a watch crystal and float around inside this hollow-heart bezel.

NECKLACE MATERIALS

1 erinite 11×7mm Swarovski crystal polygon bead

8 labradorite 3×9mm teardrops

7 garnet diamond-cut briolettes

1 rutilated 8×5mm simple-cut quartz bead

2 clear 7×9mm simple-cut quartz beads

1 polymer clay heart bezel pendant

1 pyrite 5×6mm chunk

15" (38 cm) of gold-tone 4×6mm brass cable chain

1 sterling silver 13×8mm lobster clasp

7½" (19 cm) of brass 22-gauge wire

29" (74 cm) of gold-filled 24-gauge wire

8½" (22 cm) of sterling silver 1×1mm fine cable chain

TOOLS

Wire toolbox (page 16)

FINISHED SIZE

19" (48 cm)

NECKLACE INSTRUCTIONS

1~ Cut 2½" (6.4 cm) of 4×6mm brass cable chain. Open the last link and add the silver 13×8mm lobster claw. Close the link.

2~ Use 1½" (3.8 cm) of brass 22-gauge wire to form a simple loop and attach it to the last link in the previous chain. String 1 erinite 11×7mm crystal polygon bead, form a simple loop, and attach it to 1½" (3.8 cm) of 4×6mm brass cable chain.

3~ Using 1½" (3.8 cm) of gold-filled 24-gauge wire, create a wire-wrapped dangle, strung with 1 labradorite teardrop, and attach it to the bottom simple loop in the wire-wrapped link from the previous step. Use another 1½" (3.8 cm) length of gold-filled 24-gauge wire to create another wire-wrapped dangle, strung with 1 garnet diamond-cut briolette, and attach it to the first link in the chain.

4~ Create another wire-wrapped link, using 1½" (3.8 cm) of brass 22-gauge wire, and attach it to the last link in the chain from Step 2 with a simple loop. String 1 rutilated 8×5mm quartz bead, form a simple loop, and attach to 1" (2.5 cm) of 4×6mm brass cable chain.

5~ Using 1½" (3.8 cm) of gold-filled 24-gauge wire, create a wire-wrapped dangle, strung with 1 labradorite teardrop,

and attach it to the bottom simple loop in the wire-wrapped link from the previous step. Use another 1½" (3.8 cm) length of gold-filled 24-gauge wire to create another wire-wrapped dangle, strung with 1 garnet diamond-cut briolette, and attach it to the first link in the chain.

6~ Attach 1½" (3.8 cm) of 4×6mm brass cable chain with a wire-wrapped link to the last length of chain. To create the link, use 1½" (3.8 cm) of brass 22-gauge wire and 1 quartz 7×9mm simple-cut bead. Open the last link in the chain and add the polymer clay heart bezel pendant and close the link.

7~ Using 1½" (3.8 cm) of gold-filled 24-gauge wire, create a wire-wrapped dangle, strung with 1 labradorite teardrop, and attach it to the bottom simple loop in the wire-wrapped link from the previous step. Use another 1½" (3.8 cm) length of gold-filled 24-gauge wire to create another wire-wrapped dangle, strung with 1 garnet diamond-cut briolette, and attach it to the third link down on the 4×6mm brass cable chain.

8~ Cut a 3" (7.6 cm) length of sterling silver 1×1mm cable chain. Measure down ½" (1.3 cm) on the 1×1mm cable chain and using 1" (2.5 cm) of gold-filled 24-gauge wire create a wire-wrapped link, attaching the first simple loop. Create another simple loop, attaching to the top loop in the wire-wrapped link from Step 4 (the ½" [2.5 cm] of chain will dangle freely). Measure up ½" (1.3 cm) on the remaining 2½" (6.4 cm) of 1×1mm cable chain and use 1" (2.5 cm) of gold-filled 24-gauge wire to create a wire-wrapped link, attaching the 1×1mm cable chain to the bottom loop on the wire-wrapped link from Step 5.

9~ Cut a 1½" (3.8 cm) length of sterling silver 1×1mm cable chain. Measure down ½" (1.3 cm) on the 1×1mm cable chain and use 1" (2.5 cm) of gold-filled 24-gauge wire to create a wire-wrapped link, attaching the first simple loop. Create another

simple loop, attaching to the bottom loop in the wire-wrapped link from Step 5. Measure up ½" (1.3 cm) on the remaining 1" (2.5 cm) of 1×1mm cable chain and use 1" (2.5 cm) of gold-filled 24-gauge wire to create a wire-wrapped link, attaching the 1×1mm cable chain to the fifth link up on the 4×6mm brass cable chain from the polymer clay heart bezel pendant.

10~ Using 1½" (3.8 cm) of gold-filled 24-gauge wire, create a wire-wrapped dangle, strung with 1 labradorite teardrop, and attach it to the fifth link up on the 4×6mm brass cable chain from the polymer clay heart bezel pendant.

11~ Use a 1½" (3.8 cm) length of gold-filled 24-gauge wire to create a wire-wrapped dangle, strung with 1 garnet diamond-cut briolette, and attach it to the first link of a 6" (15 cm) length of 4×6mm brass cable chain (make the simple loop slightly larger to accommodate the lobster clasp).

12~ Attach 1½" (3.8 cm) of 4×6mm brass cable chain with a wire-wrapped link to the last length of chain. To create the link, use 1½" (3.8 cm) of brass 22-gauge wire and 1 quartz 7×9mm simple-cut bead.

13~ Using 1½" (3.8 cm) of gold-filled 24-gauge wire, create a wire-wrapped dangle, strung with 1 labradorite teardrop, and attach it to the bottom simple loop in the wire-wrapped link from the previous step.

14~ Count up 5 links from the top simple loop from the wire-wrapped link from the previous step. Using 1½" (3.8 cm) of gold-filled 24-gauge wire, create a wire-wrapped dangle, strung with 1 labradorite teardrop.

15~ Count up 1 link from the wire-wrapped dangle in the previous step. Use a 1½" (3.8 cm) length of gold-filled 24-gauge wire to create a wire-wrapped dangle, strung with 1 garnet diamond-cut briolette.

16~ Count up 4 links from the garnet wire-wrapped dangle. Use a 1½" (3.8 cm) length of gold-filled 24-gauge wire to create a wire-wrapped dangle, strung with 1 labradorite teardrop.

17~ Cut a 2" (5 cm) length of sterling silver 1x1mm cable chain. Measure down ½" (1.3 cm) on the 1x1mm cable chain and, using 1" (2.5 cm) of gold-filled 24-gauge wire, create a wire-wrapped link, attaching to the first simple loop. Create another simple loop, attaching to the third link up from the wire-wrapped link from Step 12. Use 1½" (3.8 cm) of brass 22-gauge wire to form a simple loop and attach it to the last link in the chain from Step 12. String 1 pyrite 5x6mm chunk, form a simple loop, and attach it to 1" (2.5 cm) of 4x6mm brass cable chain. Use a 1½" (3.8 cm) length of gold-filled 24-gauge wire to create another wire-wrapped dangle, strung with 1 garnet diamond-cut briolette, and attach it to the bottom simple loop in the wire-wrapped link. Measure up ½" (1.3 cm) on the remaining 1½" (3.8 cm) of 1x1mm cable chain and use 1" (2.5 cm) of gold-filled 24-gauge wire to create a wire-wrapped link, attaching the 1x1mm cable chain to the second link down on the 4x6mm brass cable chain from the wire-wrapped link from Step 12.

18~ Count down 1 link from the wire-wrapped loop, attaching the 1x1mm cable chain in the previous step. Use a 1½" (3.8 cm) length of gold-filled 24-gauge wire to create a wire-wrapped dangle, strung with 1 garnet diamond-cut briolette.

19~ Count down 4 links from the wire-wrapped link from the previous step. Using 1½" (3.8 cm) of gold-filled 24-gauge wire, create a wire-wrapped dangle, strung with 1 labradorite teardrop.

20~ Cut a 2" (5 cm) length of sterling silver 1x1mm cable chain. Measure down ½" (1.3 cm) on the 1x1mm cable chain and, using 1" (2.5 cm) of gold-filled 24-gauge wire, create a wire-

wrapped link, attaching the first simple loop. Create another simple loop and attach it to the fifth link up from the wire-wrapped link from the previous step. Measure up ½" (1.3 cm) on the remaining 1½" (3.8 cm) of 1x1mm cable chain and use 1" (2.5 cm) of gold-filled 24-gauge wire to create a wire-wrapped link, attaching the 1x1mm cable chain to the second link down on the 4x6mm brass cable chain from the wire-wrapped link from Step 20.

woodland wings
NECKLACE

May 29

The woods surrounding the meadow looked dense + uninviting. Tom looked around apprehensively + I wondered aloud if something was amiss.

"Not exactly. But ORLA . . . she's not fond of humans. She protects this place + thinks all humans want to build + knock down trees."

"Like an activist?" I asked.

"Yeah, but she's not afraid to drop a boulder on a person. So don't anger her."

"Okay, so discussing what kind of wood floors I should install is not a good idea?" I received a sharp look for my cheekiness. Just then I saw the lady in question, as a FLOCK OF BUTTERFLIES filled the air. She stood before us, fanning her huge wings the color of melting snow, her hair like POLISHED OAK falling around her shoulders. When she spoke, her voice was as light as the butterflies fluttering about her.

"YOU ARE THE ONES SENT BY MIRA-BELLE?" she asked. Tom bowed + introduced us, very formally. Then she got down to business, with no hint of friendliness + no desire to chat.

"I would like a necklace, LIGHT AS A LEAF + STRONG AS STONE . . . with wings just like theirs." She put out a hand + several species perched there.

"Hmm, I'll see what I can do," I said, wondering how I was going to create the perfect piece. She ascended into the golden light, her wings glowing + sparkly.

I sat down + began to draw. I started by sketching the butterflies; THEY SEEMED TO UNDERSTAND + LANDED ON MY BOOK TO POSE. Tom took out his guitar + began playing a song that reminded me of CHAMBER MUSIC. While he played, I thought of Orla's unusual face, how her features looked so delicate + ELFIN. I imagined it would be hard to see a place you loved ravished by development.

Tom continued to play + I brought out raspberry jam tarts + coffee.

"I've been meaning to ask you about your team of ANIMAL HELPERS . . . how do you get them to do deliveries?" I asked, smiling at his rolling eyes.

"I wondered when that would come up. I was sure you were going to tell me to get a cell phone that day we went to the desert. I can talk to animals + understand them," he replied, looking intently at his tart, probably afraid to see my face.

"Really? I can see why you'd do that. Cell phones are expensive." Then we laughed, every care + trouble gone for that endless moment.

woodland wings
NECKLACE

Delicate wire-wrapped wings protected with paper and resin are reminiscent of butterfly wings. These can be time-consuming to create, so the most efficient way to make them is to create as many wire wing shapes as you will need for a few projects, because the resin coating step goes fast. Try using them for earrings—they are almost weightless and catch the light nicely. Using waterproof drawing inks, create patterns on the tissue paper before coating with resin. The tissue will vanish, but the drawings will remain.

WIRE WING MATERIALS

56" (142 cm) of black stainless steel 20-gauge wire

42" (107 cm) of brass 22-gauge wire

Glue

Tissue paper

Resin

Pearlescent powders (optional)

Gold or iridescent paint

TOOLS

Resin toolbox (page 45)

Wire cutters

Needle-nose pliers

Round-nose pliers

Craft stick

¼" (6 mm) dowel rod

Craft knife

Paintbrush

WIRE WINGS

1~ For each wing (the project calls for 8), cut a 7" (18 cm) piece of stainless steel wire. About 5" (13 cm) down, bend the wire around.

2~ Curl the wire down and, holding the end of the wire with needle-nose pliers, bend the wire into a spiral.

3~ Wrap the top piece of wire around round-nose pliers, forming a loop. Wrap the tail into another spiral and bend to lie on top of the previous spiral.

4~ Cut a 6" (15 cm) piece of brass 22-gauge wire. Wrap one end around the spiral, then wrap to the top of the wing, forming a vein. Continue wrapping the brass wire around the base wire, then form the second vein by stretching it and wrapping around the spiral. Tuck the end in.

5~ Glue down tissue paper and allow to dry, then gently tear away excess paper from the edge. Coat with resin using a craft stick. Pearlescent powders can be stirred into the resin before coating the tissue. Hang the wings onto a ¼" (6 mm) dowel rod so the resin will drip off. If there is a drip after the wing has cured, trim with a craft knife.

6~ Once the resin is set, apply gold or iridescent paint.

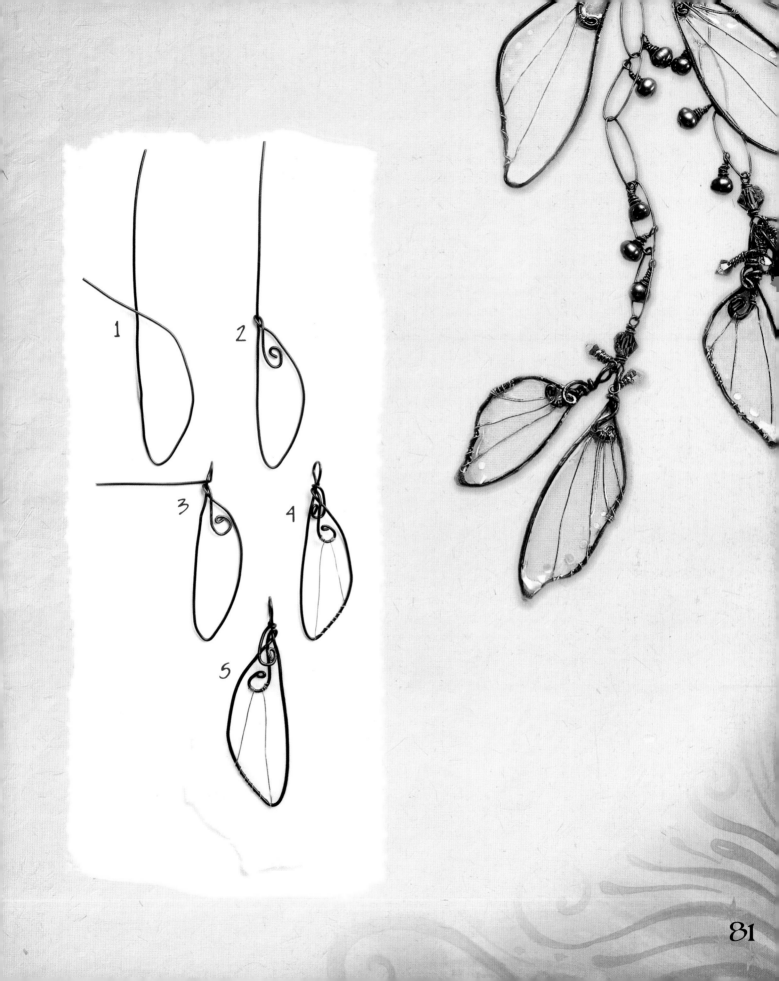

1

2

3

4

5

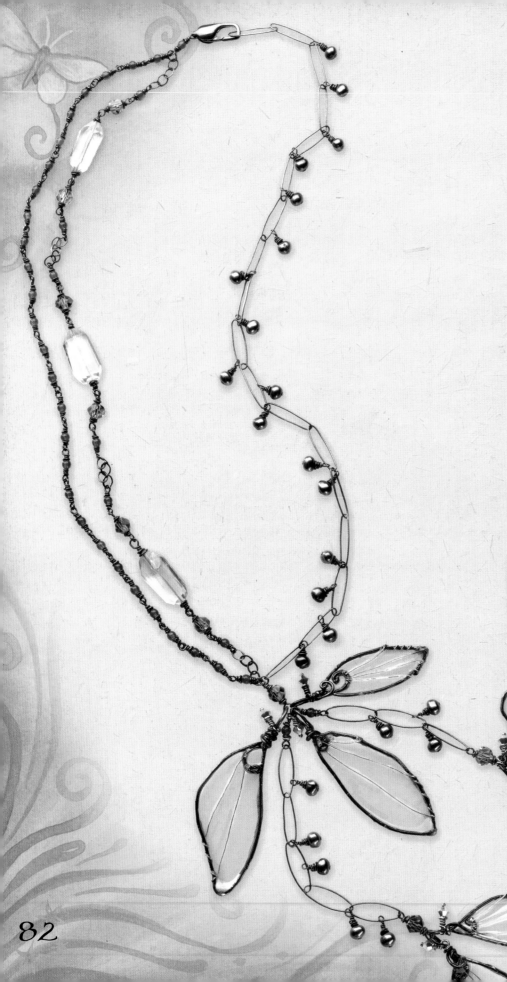

NECKLACE MATERIALS

8 rosewater opal AB×2 4mm Swarovski crystal bicones

8 wire-wrapped resin wings

36 jade 3mm rounds

25 peacock 5mm freshwater pearls

9 green 5mm faceted quartz chunks

3 green 8×21mm faceted quartz chunks

8 fine silver 1½" (3.8 cm) balled head pins

58" (147 cm) of sterling silver 24-gauge wire

17½" (44 cm) of sterling silver 4×18mm elongated oval chain

25 silver 1½" (3.8 cm) flat-head head pins

4" (10 cm) of sterling silver 4×5mm chain

1 sterling silver 7×18mm lobster clasp

TOOLS

Wire toolbox (page 16)

FINISHED SIZE

24½" (62 cm)

NECKLACE INSTRUCTIONS

1~ Use 1 balled head pin to create a wire-wrapped dangle, strung with 1 rosewater opal 4mm bicone. Attach to the bail of one wing. Repeat 7 times for all wings and set aside.

2~ Use 1½" (3.8 cm) of wire to create a wrapped loop. String 1 jade 3mm round and create another simple wire-wrapped loop. Repeat twenty-seven times, attaching the first loop to the previous, creating a wire-wrapped link chain. Set aside.

3~ Cut 12" (30 cm) of sterling silver 4×18mm elongated oval chain. Use 1 silver 1½" (3.8 cm) flat-head head pin to create a wire-wrapped dangle, strung with 1 peacock 5mm pearl, attaching to the second link in the chain. Repeat, continuing down each link of chain, sixteen times. Set aside.

4~ Repeat the above process with two additional lengths of oval chain, adding a total of 8 peacock 5mm pearls on head pins to each link. The first length of chain is 3 links long and the second is 5 links long. Use 1½" (3.8 cm) of wire to create a wrapped loop and attach it to the end of the first length of chain. String 1 green 5mm faceted quartz chunk. Create another wrapped loop, attaching to 3 resin wings. Repeat with the second length of chain, using 2 wings. Set aside.

5~ Use 1½" (3.8 cm) of wire to form a wrapped loop, attaching to ¾" (2 cm) of 4×5mm chain (5 links). String 1 jade 3mm round and form a wrapped loop. Use 11½" (3.8 cm) of wire to create a wrapped loop. String 1 green 5mm faceted quartz and make a wrapped loop. Creating a wire-wrapped chain, use 2" (5 cm) of wire to create a loop, attaching to the previous loop. String 1 green 8×21mm faceted quartz chunk and create a wrapped loop, attaching to the previous loop. Use 1½" (3.8 cm) of wire to create a wrapped loop, attaching to the previous loop. String 1 green 5mm faceted quartz and make a wrapped loop. Use 1½" (3.8 cm) of wire to form a wrapped loop, attaching the previous loop and attaching to ¾" (2 cm) of 4×5mm chain (5 links), strung with 1 jade 3mm round. Repeat this sequence twice. Add 1½" (3.8 cm) of wire to create a wrapped loop, attaching to the previous loop. String 1 green 5mm faceted quartz and make a wrapped loop. Use 1½" (3.8 cm) of wire to form a wrapped loop, attaching the previous loop and attaching to ¾" (2 cm) of 4×5mm chain (5 links).

6~ Cut 1½" (3.8 cm) of wire. Use it to create a wrapped loop, attaching to the ends of the lengths of wire-wrapped link chain from Step 2 and Step 5. String 1 jade 3mm round and create another wrapped loop, attaching to half of the sterling silver lobster clasp.

7~ Use 2" (5 cm) of wire to form a loop, attaching the ends of the lengths of wire-wrapped link chains from Step 2 and Step 5, and the chain from Step 3. String 1 green 5mm faceted quartz and form a loop, adding 1 resin wing, the first length of chain from Step 4 (3 links), 1 wing, the second length of chain from Step 4 (5 links), and 1 resin wing.

sunset
baubles
NECKLACE

May 31

OF ALL THE PLACES I'D VISITED, THIS ONE WAS MY FAVORITE. THE **CERULEAN BLUE WATER**, THE **POWDER WHITE SAND** + THE SMELL OF COCONUTS + SEAWATER ENCHANTED ME. TOM SEEMED PLEASED, TOO, SMILING HAPPILY. WE WALKED TOWARD THE FAMILY PLAYING ON THE BEACH. THEY STOOD OUT AMONG THE OTHER LOUNGERS LINED UP ALONG THE SHORE. THEY HAD HAIR THAT **GLIMMERED GREEN LIKE A BLACKBIRD'S WING**, SHIMMERY SCALES GLISTENED ON THEIR **GOLDEN BROWN SKIN**. I WONDERED WHY NO ONE NOTICED. BEFORE WE REACHED THE FAMILY, I ASKED TOM, "DOESN'T ANYBODY SEE?"

"YOU WERE GIVEN THE SIGHT, REMEMBER?" HE WHISPERED.

"THE ELDERBERRY WINE."

OH. WELL, THAT MADE SENSE.

"HELLO! I'M NIADA, THIS IS MY HUSBAND, JIM, AND MY BABIES ARE OVER THERE," SHE SAID WITH A THICK JAMAICAN ACCENT AS SHE POINTED TO THREE KIDS SPLASHING IN THE WAVES. WE INTRODUCED OURSELVES + JOINED THEM ON THE SAND.

"HEY, YOU THIRSTY?" SHE OFFERED SOME CUPS OF A COCONUT CONCOCTION. WE AC- CEPTED, AND I SIPPED THE COOL DRINK, TASTING **COCONUT + PINEAPPLE**.

"WOW, THAT'S REALLY GOOD!" I SAID, NODDING MY APPROVAL. I TOOK A BOX OF CANDIES OUT OF MY BAG + OFFERED THEM.

"THESE ARE GOOD, GIRL! YOU MAKE THEM?" I BEAMED, HAPPY MY FRUIT JELLIES WERE A HIT. THEY WERE GONE IN MINUTES, AFTER THE KIDS SAW THE BOX.

"ARE YOU GUYS LIKE MERMAIDS?" I ASKED, HOPING I DIDN'T OFFEND HER. SHE LAUGHED, TO MY RELIEF.

"WELL, WE LIKE THE WATER! WE DON'T GROW TAILS. WE'RE **NEREIDS**, OR **SEA NYMPHS** + WE CAN BREATHE UNDERWATER."

"THAT WOULD BE USEFUL!" I SAID, THINKING OF ALL THINGS I COULD SEE, ALL THE WRECKS + SUNKEN CITIES. WHAT CREATURES WERE IN THE DEEP?

WE ENJOYED CHATTING + LAUGHING WITH THE SEA NYMPHS, WATCHING THE WATER AND SEARCHING FOR SHELLS. I ASKED NIADA WHAT SHE'D LIKE ME TO MAKE FOR HER + SHE SAID, "MAYBE A NECKLACE, SOMETHING TO GO WITH MY DRESS." SHE DESCRIBED THE DRESS AS A SHEATH THAT **GRADATED FROM PEACH TO GOLD**. I THOUGHT POD SHAPES WOULD **ECHO THE FORMS OF THE SHELLS + TROPICAL FRUIT.**

WE STAYED INTO THE EVENING, WALKING UP THE BEACH TOWARD A FISH SHACK TO GET DINNER. I THOUGHT IT WOULD BE EASY TO LIVE IN PLACE LIKE THIS + THOUGHT **NIADA** WAS PRETTY LUCKY.

luelle's corsage

CUFF

June 2

Tom arrived late in the afternoon, humming to himself as he led me through the door. We stepped onto a ROOFTOP GARDEN, surrounded by industrial-looking warehouses + abandoned apartment buildings. The garden, a bright patch of green, contrasted with THE GRAY OF THE BUILDINGS. A young woman sat at a painted wicker table + chairs, watching us approach. She made a weak attempt at a smile + asked us to sit. I noticed her dress was an AMAZING PATCHWORK OF FABRICS, SEWN WITH BEADS + EMBROIDERY, the colors faded. Her pink hair, the blush color of columbines, gave her a PUNK vibe, although the color was probably natural. The word faery came to mind + I could see wings like those of a DAMSELFLY folded at her back.

"I'm LUELLE, you must be the two Mirabelle mentioned," she said politely, seeming uninterested. We told her our names + looked around the garden, feeling slightly awkward. I complimented her flowers + she seemed to wake up.

"I've had this garden since the building opened, many years ago. My husband brought me here, when I left my people. We lived downstairs," she said, looking wistful.

"Where is he now?" Tom asked. I thought I could guess + listened.

"My James has been gone a long time. I stayed with him until he was nearly NINETY years old." I realized she was much older than I thought.

"So you live here alone?" I asked, before I could stop myself.

"Yes. I miss him," I felt tears prick my eyes, then blinked them back, not wanting her to see my sadness.

We talked about her ROSES + DAHLIAS, remarking how robust everything looked. She moved like a dragonfly darting about, showing us various blooms. The plants were obviously her haven + she cared for them like children. I drew her, then the flowers, collecting information on my subject. She didn't seem to mind. Showing her garden helped her drop her guard + I found that she was funny + smart. I hoped the bracelet I imagined for her would help lift her spirits. I wondered aloud why she didn't go home to her family + she answered, "I tried to after James died, but the forest where we lived is now a golf course. I don't know what happened to them."

We continued looking at her flowers, but a sadness hung around her + it was hard not to feel for her. We left + I turned to see her looking out over the abandoned buildings, SEARCHING.

luelle's corsage
CUFF

A supple leather cuff is embellished with vintage sequins, metal clay stampings, silk flowers, and crystal beads. Leather is embroidered with ribbon, and lovely layered silk flowers are reminiscent of sacred gardens, tended with love. These comfortable cuffs can be sewn on the machine or by hand. Try cutting shapes out of the leather and backing the hole with a contrasting fabric.

FLOWER MATERIALS

Metal clay

Sewing thread

1 silver 3mm cornerless cube

1 silver 5mm daisy spacer

1 metallic 6mm round sequin

4 silk flowers

TOOLS

Metal clay toolbox (page 25)

Texturing medium (see pages 38–43 for ideas)

Flower cutter

Drink stirrer

Sewing needle

METAL CLAY FLOWERS

1— Roll out a thin sheet of metal clay and press it into a texture. Use a cutter to remove a variety of floral shapes from the sheet (two shapes per silk flower and/ or metal clay flower). Pierce a hole with a drink stirrer in the center of each shape. Fire, tumble, and patina to achieve the desired finish.

2— Stack the metal clay discs according to size, largest to smallest. Using needle and thread, secure 1 silver 3mm cornerless cube, 1 silver 5mm daisy spacer, 1 metallic 6mm round sequin, the stacked metal clay discs, and the silk flowers to the leather or cloth cuff. Pass the needle and thread through multiple times to firmly attach the centerpieces.

CUFF INSTRUCTIONS

1~ Measure two 8¼" (21 cm) lengths of the blue-green ⅜" (1 cm) wide ribbon. Using a straight stitch on your sewing machine, run a stitch down the middle of the ribbons, securing them in place along the edges of the leather. Using a zigzag stitch, sew along the edges of the ribbon to prevent the edges from flipping up. Repeat with an 8¼" (21 cm) length of crimson ¾" (2 cm) wide ribbon.

2~ Cut an 8¼" (21 cm) length of blue-green ribbon. Center the ribbon over the crimson ribbon. Using a straight stitch on your sewing machine, run a stitch down the middle of the ribbons, securing them in place. Using a zigzag stitch, sew along the edges of the ribbon to prevent the edges from flipping up.

3~ Cut two 2⅛" (5.4 cm) lengths of blue-green ribbon, the width of the cuff. Trim the edges of the cuff with the ribbon, using the same straight-stitch/zigzag technique described above.

4~ If desired, use your sewing machine to embellish the cuff with a variety of stitches to add texture.

5~ Add 3 metal clay stacked centerpieces. Using a needle and thread, embellish the cuff with sequins and cornerless cubes. Use the random design to draw focus to the middle of the cuff. Accent as much or as little as desired.

6~ Attach the metal clay button to one end of the cuff with needle and thread. Measure the cuff to your wrist and make a mark on the other side. Place the cuff on a cutting board and use a craft knife to puncture the leather, creating a buttonhole. The hole may then be embellished with a button stitch, if desired.

＊VARIATION

After firing, tumbling, and finishing the metal clay discs, add a splash of color with resin. The texture acts as reservoirs to hold the resin tinted with dyes or pigments. Be sure to allow the resin to cure completely before creating the flower embellishments.

CUFF MATERIALS

29" (74 cm) of blue-green ⅜" (1 cm) wide ribbon

1 black 8¼" wide × 2⅛" high (21 × 5.4 cm) piece of thin leather. (This can be adjusted for various wrist sizes.)

8¼" (21 cm) of crimson ¾" (2 cm) wide ribbon

3 metal clay discs (see page 114 for instructions)

4 metal clay flowers

7 metallic 6mm round sequins

9 silver 13×8mm leaf-shaped sequins

12 silver 3mm cornerless cubes

1 metal clay button with 4mm synthetic ruby (see page 31 for instructions)

2 metal clay flowers

3 silver 10×5mm Thai flowers

3 blue-green dyed 1½" (4 cm) silk flowers

1 blue-green dyed 1¾" (4.5 cm) silk flower

3 silver 5mm daisy spacers

TOOLS

Sewing machine

Needle and thread

Cutting board

Craft knife

FINISHED SIZE

8¼" W × 2⅛" H (21 cm × 54 mm)

91

the
nixie's
NECKLACE

June 3

NORMALLY, MY BEADS + COMPONENTS, CLAY + WIRE ALL HAVE THEIR BINS INSIDE AN ANTIQUE WARDROBE CABINET. NOW, BEADS WERE ON EVERY SURFACE, DRAWINGS PINNED TO THE WALL . . . . THE STUDIO PRACTICALLY HUMMED WITH CREATIVITY. WHEN TOM ARRIVED, HE GAZED AROUND + SMILED.

"I SEE YOU'RE WORKING HARD," HE REMARKED, WHILE HOLDING UP A NECKLACE.

"WHERE ARE WE GOING TODAY, TOM?" I ASKED.

"TODAY WE ARE GOING TO A VERY OLD FOREST NEAR INVERNESS," HE SAID + I HEARD HIS ACCENT THICKEN.

"WHERE ARE YOU FROM?" "OH, ALL AROUND. I'VE LIVED IN MANY PLACES. BUT SCOTLAND IS WHERE I WAS BORN."

"I SEE. THEN IT'S HOME FOR YOU," I SAID, FEELING SURPRISINGLY PLEASED TO SEE HIS ROOTS.

"YES, WELL, LET'S GO THEN" + HE OPENED A DOORWAY.

THE TREES WERE LARGE + DEEP GREEN, SHADING THE LEAF-STREWN EARTH. WE STOOD FOR A MOMENT, DECIDING WHAT TO DO. TOM SEEMED UNCERTAIN, BUT THEN SAID, "I THINK IT'S THIS WAY" + WE VENTURED IN DEEPER.

I BECAME AWARE OF LARGE INSECTS FLYING AROUND + REALIZED THEY WERE WINGED PEOPLE THE SIZE OF MY FINGER. I MARVELED AT THEIR TINY CLOTHES OF SPIDER SILK, LILY PETALS + AN ASSORTMENT OF OTHER NATURAL MATERIALS. I WANTED TO CATCH ONE + KEEP IT, BUT I DIDN'T THINK THAT WOULD HAPPEN. WE ARRIVED AT A CLEAR POOL OF WATER, RINGED WITH STONES, SUNLIGHT FILTERING THROUGH THE LEAVES + CASTING PATTERNS OVER THE SURFACE. A HEAD BROKE THROUGH THE WATER + WE GREETED THE NIXIE AS SHE SWAM TOWARD US.

"HELLO, THERE," SHE SAID IN A SINGSONG, HEAVILY ACCENTED VOICE. HER HAIR LOOKED GREEN-GOLD, WITH LITTLE WATER LILIES + PEARLS WOVEN THROUGH THE STRANDS. I KNEW WHEN I SAW HOW SHE DECORATED HER HAIR, WHAT I WOULD MAKE FOR HER. WE EXCHANGED POLITE NICETIES FOR A WHILE + I ASKED HER WHERE SHE LIVED.

"OH, I LIVE HERE! SEE, STRAIGHT DOWN THERE, THAT'S MY HOUSE." SHE MOTIONED TO THE BOTTOM OF THE POOL + WE PEERED INTO THE WATER. AT THE BOTTOM I COULD SEE A STONE HOUSE, ROUNDED + SMOOTH, WITH A FRONT GARDEN, FILLED WITH STRANGE BLOOMING PLANTS. I IMAGINED MYSELF IN THE COOL, AQUATIC WORLD, HOW THE LIGHT MUST LOOK, TINTED BLUE-GREEN WITH SILVERY FISH SWIMMING BY, LIKE BIRDS IN THE SKY. WE STAYED FOR A LITTLE LONGER, SITTING BY THE WATER'S EDGE, WHILE I DREW. I NOTICED MY SHADOW LOOKED ODD, THEN SAW THE REASON FOR THE SHAPE ON MY SHOULDER. HIDING IN MY HAIR SAT A LOVELY FAIRY WITH LUNA MOTH WINGS + DARK TEAL HAIR. THE NIXIE THOUGHT IT WAS A VERY GOOD OMEN THAT THE FAIR FOLK WOULD COME THAT CLOSE. I THOUGHT SHE MIGHT BE RIGHT.

the nixie's NECKLACE

Sinuous vines shaped from metal clay and bound with wire-wrapped crystals and lustrous freshwater pearls have the feel of a magical forest. The beautiful links can be used as earrings—just add hooks to one end and dangle stones or pearls from the opposite loop. The links can also be dried over a rounded form to give them a nice bend for a bracelet component. Substitute the vintage Lucite seaweed leaves with modified resin-coated wire wings from the Woodland Wings project on page 78. Instead of wing shapes, form leaf shapes and tint the resin green with dyes or pigments.

VINE LINK MATERIALS

Metal clay

Slip

TOOLS

Metal clay toolbox (page 25)

Small paintbrush

PMC VINE LINKS

1— Divide the pack of metal clay into 6 round ½" (1.3 cm) balls. Working one at a time (keeping the others covered so they don't dry out), roll the balls into thin logs ¼" (6 mm) thick, tapering to blunt points.

2— Curl the ends into loops, wrapping the ends around.

3— Secure the loop by painting with slip, making sure there are no gaps.

4— Place on a heating plate until the links are bone dry. Check for cracks and fill areas as necessary with more slip.

5— Allow the links to dry completely, and then fire. Tumble and patina. Buff with a polishing cloth as desired.

3

10 green 5mm faceted
quartz chunks

6 metal clay vine links

23 irregular 7×4mm heishi
pearls

1 irregular 16×14mm pearl

3 vintage Lucite 40×15mm
seaweed leaves

5½' (1 m 67 cm) of silver
24-gauge wire

1 sterling silver 27×14mm toggle
clasp

1½" (4 cm) of silver 4×6mm
cable chain

7 silver 1½" (3.8 cm) head pins

TOOLS

Wire toolbox (page 16)

FINISHED SIZE

19¾" (50.2 cm)

NECKLACE INSTRUCTIONS

1— Use 4" (10 cm) of wire to form a fancy-wrapped
loop. Attach to one half of the clasp. String 1 green
5mm quartz chunk and form another fancy-
wrapped loop. Attach to 1 metal clay vine link.

2— Use 4" (10 cm) of wire to form a fancy-wrapped
loop. Attach to the metal clay vine link. String
1 green 5mm quartz chunk and form a fancy-
wrapped loop. Attach to a metal clay vine link. Repeat four times, forming a chain of fancy-wrapped
links and metal clay vine links.

3— Use 1½" (4 cm) of wire to form a simple loop. Attach
to the remaining half of the clasp. String 1 irregular
7×4mm heishi pearl and form another wrapped
loop. Use 1½" (4 cm) of wire to form a simple
loop. Attach to the previous loop. String 1 irregular
7×4mm heishi pearl and close with a simple loop.
Repeat eighteen times, connecting to the previous
links, forming a wire-wrapped link chain.

4— Use 2" (5 cm) of wire to form a fancy-wrapped
loop. Attach the end of the wire-wrapped irregular
heishi pearl link chain and the metal clay vine and
green 5mm faceted quartz chunks chain. String 1
green 5mm faceted quartz chunk and form another
fancy-wrapped loop. Attach to 1½" (4 cm) of 4×6
cable chain.

5— Embellish the chain with wire-wrapped head pins
to form a tassel: Use 1 head pin to form a fancy-
wrapped dangle with the irregular pearl. Attach to

the first link. Use 2" (5 cm) of silver 24-gauge wire
to form a fancy-wrapped dangle with 1 Lucite leaf
on the second link. Continue to the third link with a
wire-wrapped dangle with 1 head pin and 1 irregular
7×4mm heishi pearl. For the next link, attach 1 head
pin made up into a wire-wrapped dangle with 1 green
5mm faceted quartz chunk. Use 2" (5 cm) of wire to
form a fancy-wrapped dangle, strung with 1 Lucite
leaf. Attach to the next link. Add another irregular
7×4mm heishi pearl wire-wrapped dangle to the next
link, using 1 head pin. Use 1 head pin to create a wire-
wrapped dangle with 1 green 5mm faceted quartz
chunk. Attach to the next link. Skip the next link. Use
2" (5 cm) of wire to create a wire-wrapped dangle
with 1 vintage Lucite leaf. Attach to the next link.
Skip the next link. Use 1 head pin to create a fancy-
wrapped dangle with 1 irregular 7×4mm heishi pearl.
Attach to the next-to-last link. For the last link in the
chain, use 1 head pin to attach 1 green 5mm faceted
quartz chunk in a fancy-wrapped dangle.

6— Prepare a liver of sulfur solution. Dip and wash the
piece until appropriately darkened. Polish with a
polishing cloth. This will bring out the details in the
wirework.

*VARIATION

A beautiful luna
moth pendant
looks wonderful
hanging from the
metal clay vines
as well.

dogwood
NECKLACE

June 5

When Tom arrived, I was ready for our next adventure. I baked honey cakes and made a sweet tea of chamomile + milk. He had his guitar and the travel box. He opened it onto a beautiful woodland, with lilies blooming under the trees. I could see tall, skinny trees, some that looked like birch, others I didn't know. We walked in a comfortable silence, admiring the scenery. He stopped at a DOGWOOD + waited. Apparently, this was our stop.

"So, where's our friend," I said looking around.

"In here," he said, pointing at the tree. He placed his hand on the smooth bark + the tree trembled, as if shook by a breeze. Then, a face appeared in the trunk. She looked at us with sleepy eyes and a dazed expression.

"Yes?" she asked, sinking a little into the bark.

"Hello, we're the friends that Mirabelle sent." Tom continued the introductions + she sank a further inch.

"Would you mind terribly, if you came out to talk?" asked Tom.

"I would mind . . . but I suppose I have to," the HAMADRYAD said sulkily. She emerged, faster than I imagined + I found myself staring at a SLENDER, WAIFLIKE GIRL WITH DOGWOOD BLOOMS + leaves sprouting from her head. Her dusky skin had a greenish cast, like wood with the bark stripped back. Her shift seemed to be made out of a BARK FABRIC, but lightweight + silky.

"OKAY, HERE I AM," she said gloomily, leaning against her tree.

I asked my usual questions, hoping I could put her at ease. I learned that her tree was THE MOST BEAUTIFUL + NOBLE TREE anywhere + that she couldn't be happier with it. I almost asked how many bedrooms + if it was cold in the winter, but didn't think that would help. She allowed me to draw her, examining the picture when I finished it.

"Hmmm, this is good. I like it. You've drawn my tree very regally," the Hamadryad said, smiling at me for the first time. We let her go back to her tree + she did so without hesitation, but told us "it was nice" as she sank in. Left to our own devices, we wandered around searching for a good place to picnic. We found a large oak on a hill covered with clover, so we sat beneath it + talked + ate the honey cakes.

"How old are you, Tom" I asked, around a mouthful of cake.

"OLDER THAN YOU," he said slyly + picked up his guitar.

"Come on, you can't be older than twenty-five!" I said, studying him closer, his hair was thick + dark, his tan skin unlined around his dark blue eyes.

"I was born in 1220," + he smiled his lopsided grin & played a modern song by Dave Matthews Band. I stared, my mouth almost forgetting to chew.

"You are teasing!" I said + threw a handful of clover at him. He brushed it aside and said, "You're right. I'm twenty-five. Anything else you'd like to know?" I couldn't bring myself to ask the one question I was dying to know. Maybe some other time. I laughed + poured us more tea.

dogwood NECKLACE

Silver branches and blossoms are bound to crystals and pearls in this lovely necklace. The delicate blossoms are the product of polymer templates that are used to cut shapes from metal clay.

METAL CLAY BRANCHES, FLOWERS, & LEAVES MATERIALS

Metal clay

Slip

Polymer clay

TOOLS

Metal clay toolbox (page 25)

Polymer clay toolbox (page 20)

Texture stamp (see page 40 for instructions)

Texture pod (see page 39 for instructions)

Pointed tool

Craft knife

Coffee stirrer

Wooden tool

METAL CLAY BRANCH LINKS

1— To create a 1" (2.5 cm) branch link, roll out a tube of clay, ¼" (6 mm) thick, on a texture stamp using another texture plate to roll it out—this provides continuous impressions, with no flat spots from fingers. Use a pointed tool to poke holes on both ends of the branch. Make 8 branch links.

2— Place on a hot plate. While on the plate, dot with slip to create tiny balls on the surface. These bubbles will pop and create little divots, resembling knotholes in bark.

3— Allow the links to dry completely. Fire, tumble, and patina.

METAL CLAY FLOWERS + LEAVES

1— Make a pattern by rolling out a sheet of polymer clay. Trace a flower and leaf designs into the clay and cut them out (make 3 flowers and 8 leaves). Follow the manufacturer's instructions to bake the polymer patterns until hard. This pattern is reusable.

2— Roll out metal clay into a thin sheet and use the polymer clay patterns to trace designs. Following the pattern, use a craft knife to cut out metal clay flowers and leaves. Poke stringing holes with a coffee stirrer and carve detail lines with a wooden tool. Allow to dry completely.

3— Fire and tumble. Patina as desired.

NECKLACE INSTRUCTIONS

1— Cut a 2" (5 cm) length of silver 5mm round chain. Use 2" (5 cm) silver 22-gauge wire to create a fancy-wrapped loop, attaching to the end of the chain. String 1 padparadscha 4mm crystal-encrusted rondelle, attaching the fancy-wrapped loop to the end of 1 metal clay 43×4mm link.

2— Use 2" (5 cm) silver 22-gauge wire to create a fancy-wrapped loop, attaching to the metal clay link from the previous step. String 1 padparadscha 4mm crystal-encrusted rondelle, attaching the fancy-wrapped loop to the end of another metal clay 43×4mm link. Repeat twice, attaching to the previous link, creating a fancy wire-wrap and metal clay link chain. Set aside.

3— For the other half of the necklace, use 2" (5 cm) silver 22-gauge wire to create a fancy-wrapped loop, attaching to the silver 12×7mm S clasp. String 1 padparadscha 4mm crystal-encrusted rondelle, attaching the fancy-wrapped loop to the end of 1 metal clay 43×4mm link. Use 2" (5 cm) of silver 22-gauge wire to create a fancy-wrapped loop, attaching to the metal clay link from the previous step. String 1 padparadscha 4mm crystal-encrusted rondelle, attaching the fancy-wrapped loop to the end of another metal clay 43×4mm link. Repeat twice, attaching to the previous link, creating a fancy wire-wrap and metal clay link chain.

4— Cut a 2" (5 cm) length of silver 5mm round chain. Use 2" (5 cm) of silver 22-gauge wire to create a fancy-wrapped loop, attaching to the end of the chain. String 1 padparadscha 4mm crystal-encrusted rondelle, attaching the fancy-wrapped loop to the end of the last metal clay 43×4mm link from the previous step. Use another 2" (5 cm) of silver 22-gauge wire to create a fancy-wrapped loop, attaching to the top link of the chain (already attached to the other half of the necklace). String 1 padparadscha 4mm crystal-encrusted rondelle, attaching the fancy-wrapped loop to the end of the last metal clay 43×4mm link from Step 2.

5— Use 1 balled head pin to create a fancy-wrapped dangle. Stack 1 golden shadow 4mm Swarovski crystal sequin, 1 bronze 7mm daisy spacer, 1 metal clay 18mm flower, attaching to the first link in the 5mm round chain. Repeat, adding 2 metal clay fancy-wrapped flower dangles to the fourth and last links of chain.

6— Using 7 silver 5mm jump rings, add metal clay 12×19mm leaves to the outside of the middle 2 metal clay 43×4mm branch links. Add 2 more to the top link of round chain and 1 to the sixth and seventh link down.

7— Wire wrap the pearls and crystals between the flowers and links, evenly spacing them along the chain.

8— Use a jump ring to add the fine-gauge silver chain, attaching it to last link of round silver chain with one side longer than the other.

9— Dip the necklace into liver of sulfur to patina it.

NECKLACE MATERIALS

8 metal clay 43×4mm branches

4" (10 cm) of 5mm round silver chain

8 padparadscha 4mm Swarovski crystal-encrusted rondelles

5' (152 cm) silver 22-gauge wire

1 silver 12×7mm S clasp

6 silver 12×19mm leaves

3 silver 18mm flowers

5 irregular 7×4mm heishi freshwater pearls

8 golden shadow 4mm Swarovski crystal sequins

5 satin rose 6mm Swarovski crystal bicones

3 bronze 7mm flower spacers

2" (5 cm) of 2×3mm fine silver chain

3 silver 1½" (38 mm) ball-end head pins

7 silver 5mm jump rings

10 silver 1½" (38 mm) fine 24-gauge head pins

TOOLS

Wire toolbox (page 16)

FINISHED SIZE

18½" (47 cm)

time + memory
NECKLACE

June 7

The days flew by. I could hardly believe how many places I'd been to. I wondered what my life would be like when this project was finished. I shuddered + waited for Tom.

I looked around at the BRILLIANT GREEN of the hills + at the ocean far below. Tom offered his arm as we walked down a steep hill; otherwise, I might have fallen—the fault either my footing or my skipping heart. As we made our way to the shore, Tom told me a little about Tuala.

"SHE IS A SELKIE, a fey creature that wears a seal skin to become a seal. If her skin is stolen, she belongs to the one who has it. She was happy with the man who kept her skin for a while, but then she pined for the sea. She had children to occupy her, but the desire was in her bones."

"SO WHAT HAPPENED?"

I asked, eager for the rest.

"Well, her man died, without telling her where her skin was + she was forced to endure many more years before she found it. She went to the sea + has come out as a woman only a handful of times."

"Then this is a big deal for her to meet us."

"Yes, it is. I hope she comes out."

AND THEN WE SAW HER.

A seal head popped out of the waves + watched us before diving under.

A moment later another head emerged, DARK HAIR slicked against her pale face, eyes luminous + large. She walked stiffly toward us, as if unsure how to use her legs. She had her SPOTTED SKIN draped over her body, clutched in her white hands. She attempted to speak, emitting short barks, then tried again, in an old language, thick sounding + unknown to me. Tom whispered something to her, calming her. She smiled then, ruefully, perhaps embarrassed.

I asked Tom to ask her my questions about what she'd like. As they spoke, she stopped to pick up a stone, then handed it to me, smiling + saying something I couldn't understand. Tom translated:

"IT'S A GARNET, FOR YOU."

I smiled + thanked her. She collected lots of tiny stones while we talked, and I drew many pictures of her, the water, other seals that played nearby, + one of Tom. Before we left, she surprised me by taking my hand in her cold one + dropping more pebbles into it, then she gave me a one-armed hug. Tom looked amused at my expression of shock; I was rarely, if ever, hugged by almost-naked selkies. Then he said, "You remind her of someone she knew a long time ago."

time+ memory
NECKLACE

Silver-capped hollow glass beads enclose a collection of rare stones and sparkly gems. Necklaces such as this are perfect for encapsulating treasured goods. These amulets are also a beautiful way to protect a small picture or drawing, preserving the tiny image, yet still showcasing it.

BEAD CAP MATERIALS

Metal clay

Large hollow glass beads

Slip

TOOLS

Metal clay toolbox (page 25)

Texture plate (optional)

Straw

Pointed tool (optional)

Doming block (optional)

BEAD CAPS

1— Start with a small ball of metal clay, smaller than a pea, to make one cap for a bead that is 1" (2.5 cm) or more in diameter (this project will require 12 caps). Create a round disc by pressing the metal clay flat with your fingers or with something textured, if desired. With a straw, poke a hole in the center, a little larger than you want the finished size hole to be. Remember not to make it too large if you plan to cover a large bead hole; otherwise, all the inclusions will fall out between the bead and the cap.

2— Press the disc of metal clay onto the bead and decorate it with balls of metal clay attached with slip or use a pointed tool to inscribe a design on the surface. Repeat Steps 1 and 2 for the other side of the bead.

3— When dry, gently remove the caps from the beads. Fire and finish. They will come out smaller, but still fit your bead. If they are too small, use a doming block to adjust for the shrinkage.

1

NECKLACE MATERIALS

6 hollow beads with caps for each end

Tiny gems and crystals to fit inside beads (no larger than the opening of the hollow beads)

32" (81 cm) of silver 22-gauge wire

Seven 3" (7.6 cm) lengths of silver 6mm oval chain

Scotch tape

1 silver 8×18mm snake hook

TOOLS

Wire toolbox (page 16)

FINISHED SIZE

32½" (83 cm)

NECKLACE INSTRUCTIONS

1~ Use 5" (13 cm) of wire to create a fancy-wrapped loop, attaching one length of chain. Repeat five times.

2~ Fill the hollow beads with tiny gems. Tape the caps to the ends so nothing falls out.

3~ Add 1 bead to each piece of wire. Wrap the other end, placing another length of chain through the loop.

4~ Continue wrapping chains to loops that are wrapped at the ends of each bead until all hollow beads have been used.

5~ Use 2" (5 cm) of silver 22-gauge wire to attach the hook to the last link.

tiny treasures to cherish

You can encapsulate just about any small item within the glass beads. Look for objects with interesting colors and textures that are dried and won't shrivel up later (don't use anything fresh, such as flowers or leaves). Try drawing on pieces of parchment or painting on wet-media acetate, which will make the painting appear to float within the bead—the acetate will virtually disappear once inside (just be sure to wipe off any fingerprints). You can also include small drawings, messages, or snippets of poetry on tiny pieces of rice paper or other decorative papers.

riverbed
RINGS

June 9

We stood near an enormous waterfall, waiting for one of the fair folk to approach. Tom + I gazed at it for a few moments, then began to argue about whether to wait or walk around. He thought it would be more interesting to see the area, claiming she could find us by scent + I said, why make it difficult? We didn't notice the RED FOX watching us from a rock above our heads until we heard it chuckle. It leaped to the ground + shimmered like a mirage + then a woman stood where the fox had been.

"That was amazing!" I gasped + studied the fox-woman closely. Her hair was the same red as the fox's fur + her eyes, a HONEY BROWN, were watching us with amusement.

"I hope I'm not interrupting?" she smiled. I was surprised to hear she sounded American, with no trace of the exotic.

"No, of course not," I shot Tom a superior look. "So, how do you like my home?" she asked amiably.

"I think it's very beautiful. Have you lived here long?" I asked, as we began to walk along the bank, following her away from the waterfall.

"Five or six years. I used to live in the Midwest, but it started getting crowded. + it's flat," she smirked.

"THE OREGON COAST isn't short of beauty," Tom threw in.

"No, it's not . . . . . how about we stop here," she gestured to a SUNNY SPOT along the bank, where the water moved slower. She crept to the edge, her movements lithe + unnaturally graceful, as she picked up RIVER STONES.

"I brought some Mexican chocolate cookies + rice tea. Would you like some?" I asked + was pleased to see her expression of utter happiness.

"Yes, please! It's been an age since I've tasted CHOCOLATE!" her share disappeared with sounds of pleasure. She praised my abilities in the kitchen + said she never had the skills. I realized that she wasn't just a forest-dwelling shape-shifter, but had also lived as a human.

"Okay, people, time to skip stones!" with that, she tossed a flat pebble + we watched it bounce five times before sinking.

"Watch this!" said Tom, flicking a stone that bounced eight times. I tossed the next one + it plopped right in. Everyone laughed + proceeded to give me instructions on how to hold the rock + the wrist action necessary for the most skips. We continued tossing pebbles + talking until late afternoon. I watched her pluck petals from a BUTTERCUP + drop them into the water. They drifted slowly away, bright SPOTS of YELLOW against the rusty shades of RIVER STONES. I sketched her + the stones, the lemon yellow petals + the fox that she would change into when we left.

105

riverbed RINGS

Stones sparkle from a bed of silver, as leaves and pebbles skip along the surface. These are quick to make and look like lost relics. For a variation, try hammering the bands or wrapping two widths of wire for a rustic effect. The best part is not having to account for shrinkage in the bands!

RING MATERIALS

2¼" (6 cm) of fine silver
18-gauge wire (for a size 7 ring)

¾" (2 cm) ball of metal clay

Synthetic stones that
can be fired

Slip

Fine silver 22-gauge wire
jump rings (1 per ring) (page 17)

6" (15 cm) of silver 22-gauge wire

TOOLS

Metal clay toolbox (page 25)

Wire toolbox (page 16)

Ring mandrel

Sandpaper (300 grit)

Toothpick

FINISHED SIZE

Size 7 ring

*VARIATION

For a thicker band or a stacked look, use multiple fine silver wire ring shanks. Simply apply slip to the joints.

1

2

3

RING INSTRUCTIONS

1~ Cut the fine silver 18-gauge wire and bend it around a ring mandrel (if a ring mandrel is not available, use something with similar dimensions, such as a dowel rod or thick marker). The ring doesn't have to close and can have a gap—it will be covered with metal clay. Don't worry if it is not perfect. Use a small amount of (300-grit) sandpaper to abrade the joint where the two ends of the fine silver wire meet.

2~ Press some of the metal clay around the wire, enclosing the joint completely and shaping the base for the stones. Blend the metal clay into the wire, removing the seam. Allow to dry. Brush on some slip after drying around the areas where the wire and metal clay join. During firing, the slip, metal clay, and fine silver wire ring shank will fuse together.

3~ Using stone-setting techniques (see pages 32–34), set the stones in place, using a wet paintbrush to make a slurry so the metal clay will stick to the dry metal clay base.

4~ Place a jump ring between the stones, wiggling it back and forth to make sure it grabs. Add small dry metal clay balls for more decoration and allow it to dry.

5~ Make tiny dangles by pressing metal clay into tiny molds or roll out the metal clay and cut out little shapes. Use a toothpick to make holes.

6~ Fire and polish. Wire wrap stones and dangles to the ring, making sure they aren't too long, which can be bothersome when wearing.

urban faery EARRINGS

June 9

I FOUND MYSELF STARING OUT AT CENTRAL PARK FROM MY LIVING ROOM. I COULD SEE WE WOULD ENTER UNNOTICED, FROM OUR POSITION BEHIND A STAND OF TREES. TOM SEEMED EXCITED TO GO, SO WE WENT THROUGH + I WAS HIT WITH THE SOUNDS + SMELLS OF THE CITY. I COULD HEAR CAR HORNS, DUCKS SQUAWKING + BIKE BELLS. THE SMELL OF EXHAUST, GARBAGE + STALE PERFUME CONTRASTED WITH THE BEAUTY OF THE PARK.

WE WALKED TO THE BETHESDA FOUNTAIN TO WAIT FOR OUR NEXT SUBJECT + TALKED ABOUT HOW CROWDED IT WAS + WHAT WE COULD DO AFTER OUR MEETING. I LISTED SEVERAL MUSEUMS + AN ART SUPPLY SHOP FAMOUS FOR STOCKING EVERYTHING. HE LISTED A RECORD STORE + SOMEPLACE TO EAT. WE SAT ON A PARK BENCH + WAITED. A FEW MOMENTS LATER WE WERE IN THE COMPANY OF A VERY BEAUTIFUL WOMAN, WITH PLATINUM HAIR, COBALT BLUE EYES, A WILLOWY THIN FIGURE + SLIGHTLY POINTED EARS. I THOUGHT I RECOGNIZED HER FROM AN AD FOR JEANS, EVEN WITHOUT HER DISGUISE FOR MORTALS. TOM TRIED NOT TO STARE. I FOUND HIS REACTION INCREDIBLY ANNOYING + WANTED TO LEAVE THAT SECOND.

SHE BEGAN TO CHATTER LIKE A SONGBIRD ABOUT MIRABELLE, WHAT I SHOULD MAKE, WHAT MIRABELLE WAS WEARING . . . I SAT BACK WITH MY SKETCHBOOK + MARVELED AT HOW EASY THIS WAS GOING TO BE. SHE REMARKED HOW MUCH SHE LIKED THE CARVINGS AROUND THE PAVILION, ESPECIALLY THE ONES WITH FLOWERS + BIRDS, SO I SKETCHED THOSE, TOO.

AFTER WHAT SEEMED LIKE A LONG TIME, I GOT UP STIFFLY + THANKED HER FOR HER TIME. THEN TO MY UTTER AMAZEMENT, SHE OFFERED TO TAKE US AROUND THE CITY! I GLANCED AT TOM, WHO WAS CLEARLY DONE WITH HIS EARLY REACTION + HE SEEMED TO SHAKE HIS HEAD NO. SHE CONTINUED TO TALK + WE FOLLOWED HER THROUGH THE PARK. WE WALKED AT A QUICK PACE, STOPPING TO GET DRINKS + COOKIES. SHE PROVED TO BE AN EXCELLENT GUIDE, SHOWING US ALL OVER THE CITY TO HIDDEN GEMS, INCLUDING THE DUSTY STORE THAT SOLD PAINT PIGMENTS, THE WALLS LINED WITH HUNDREDS OF JARS OF COLORS. SHE FOUND TOM A RECORD STORE THAT CARRIED OBSCURE BANDS + ALSO VERY OLD IRISH BALLADS.

WHEN EVENING ROLLED AROUND, SHE INVITED US TO A PARTY, BUT YOU NEEDED TO BE FEY TO GET IN. WE DECLINED + TOM AND I MADE OUR WAY TO A THAI RESTAURANT, WHERE WE ORDERED ENOUGH FOOD FOR THREE + POLISHED IT OFF BEFORE ASKING FOR MANGO + SWEET RICE. I THOUGHT ABOUT THE ELF WOMAN AND HER SONGBIRD CHATTER + SMILED. I LIKED HER + COULDN'T WAIT TO MAKE HER JEWELRY.

urban faery
EARRINGS

Carved stamps were used to provide the detail, which mimics stone carvings, in the silver hoops. They are the perfect way to showcase faceted stones. These pieces can be used as gorgeous clasps—just make a stamped toggle bar to fit the hole.

HOOP MATERIALS
Metal clay
Olive oil

TOOLS
Metal clay toolbox (page 25)
Circle cutters (3 cm and 1.6 cm)
Texture stamp
Cutting surface
Straw
Polishing cloth

METAL CLAY HOOPS

1— Carve a stamp (see page 41 for instructions) using two circle cutters, one for the perimeter (3 cm) and one for the interior hole (1.6 cm), as guidelines to keep the design within. Using cutters for outlines on the stamp will make it easier to cut out the holes of the pressing from the stamp.

2— Roll the metal clay into two balls to create a set of earrings. Lightly cover the stamp with olive oil so the clay will release. Press firmly into the center of the stamp and out toward the edge. This method (rather than rolling a sheet out and pressing the stamp into the sheet) produces much finer detail because the clay is forced into all of the design's recesses.

3— Lay the pressed image on a cutting surface and use the cutters to refine the shape of the outside and to remove the middle. With a straw, poke 5 holes at the bottom for dangles and 1 hole at the top for the ear wire and center dangle.

4— Allow to dry. Fire and polish.

EARRING MATERIALS

2 garnet 9×8mm briolettes

10 andalucite 6×8mm briolettes

2 metal clay pendants

25" (64 cm) of silver 26-gauge wire

2 Bali silver 13×11mm ball ear wires

TOOLS

Wire toolbox (page 16)

FINISHED SIZE

2" (51 mm)—from the top of the ear wire to the bottom dangle

EARRING INSTRUCTIONS

1~ Use 2½" (6.4 cm) of silver 26-gauge wire to create a fancy-wrapped dangle strung with 1 garnet 9×8 briolette. Attach at the top hole so that the dangle hangs in the center of the interior hole. Carefully add an ear wire to the same hole.

2~ Create a fancy-wrapped dangle strung with 1 andalucite 6×8 briolette with 2" (5 cm) of silver 26-gauge wire. Attach the dangle to a bottom hole in the metal clay hoop. Repeat four times for the remaining holes along the bottom.

3~ Repeat both steps for the second earring.

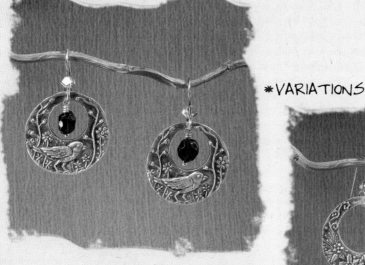

*VARIATIONS

Make several size stamps that align with one another and stack for a layered look. For additional contrast, patina each layer differently.

lila's garden
NECKLACE

June 10

THE WILDFLOWER MEADOW WE WALKED THROUGH CONTAINED A VAST ASSORTMENT OF SPECIMENS: HIMALAYAN BLUE POPPIES, INDIGO DELPHINIUMS, DEEP PINK COLUMBINES, + SNAPDRAGONS IN EVERY HUE. LUCKILY, THE STONE PATH KEPT US FROM TRODDING ON THE FLOWERS ON THE WAY TO THE UNUSUAL STICK- + VINE-COVERED HOUSE. IT LOOKED LIKE AN ENORMOUS OVERTURNED BASKET, WITH FLOWERS CREEPING UP THE SIDES, WINDOWS, AND DOOR.

A SHORT FIGURE APPEARED WEARING WIDE PANTS + A PINAFORE IN LINEN. SHE WALKED TOWARD US + I SAW SHE HAD TRANSPARENT WINGS FOLDED AT HER BACK, LIKE THE GLOSSY ONES ON BEES. HER PRETTY FACE HELD SLANTED GOLD EYES + SKIN DUSTED WITH FRECKLES. WE EXCHANGED GREETINGS. WE DISCOVERED HER NAME WAS LILA + THAT SHE WAS A GARDENER.

"HOW ARE THINGS GROWING, LILA?" TOM ASKED POLITELY.

"MY WILDFLOWERS ARE WONDERFUL, BUT MY STRAWBERRIES LOOK WEAK. MY ROSES ARE BLOOMING + I HOPE I GET A LOT. . . ." SHE CONTINUED FOR A WHILE, THOROUGHLY EXPLAINING WHICH PLANTS PLEASED HER + WHICH DIDN'T. SHE TOLD US ABOUT A ROSE JAM SHE HOPED TO MAKE + A RASPBERRY MEAD (IF THE VINES WERE GENEROUS THIS YEAR). I PRODUCED MY SKETCHBOOK AND DREW QUICK SKETCHES OF PLANTS + OF LILA, WHO FLITTED FROM PLANT TO SHRUB, JUST LIKE A BUMBLEBEE.

OCCASIONALLY SHE STOPPED + EXAMINED MY DRAWINGS, NODDING IN APPROVAL. I JOTTED DOWN HER FAVORITE FLOWERS, MAKING NOTES ABOUT COLORS. SHE WAS MUMBLING SOMETHING ABOUT HOW FEW BEES THERE WERE THIS YEAR, A PROBABLE REASON FOR HER SMALLER YIELD.

I GAZED AROUND IN AMAZEMENT. I COULDN'T IMAGINE A MORE BEAUTIFUL GARDEN. SHE ASKED ME IF I LIKED TO PRESS FLOWERS, THEN HANDED ME A PINK DAISY. I LAID IT IN THE BACK OF MY BOOK + FLATTENED IT. WE CONTINUED PRESSING SMALL FLOWERS UNTIL MY BOOK BULGED WITH PERFECT INSPIRATION FOR HER PIECE.

LILA SAID, "LOOK AT YOU! COVERED IN FAIRIES!"

I LOOKED AT MYSELF + SAW THAT I WAS, INDEED, COVERED. THEY WERE DISGUISED AS FLOWERS, THEIR LITTLE FACES + WINGS TINTED WITH THE COLORS OF THE SURROUNDING SPECIMENS. I TOUCHED ONE AND IT CLUNG TO MY FINGER, SO I SET IT ON MY BOOK + SKETCHED IT. THE OTHERS FLEW UP TO SEE MY DRAWING, THEN SETTLED AROUND ME, TAKING TURNS POSING. IT WAS SOMETHING I'D NEVER FORGET. LILA'S MEADOW WAS A PEACEFUL PLACE + I ENJOYED WANDERING THROUGH HER GARDEN. WE PREPARED TO GO + SHE PRESENTED US WITH TWO BIG JARS OF LAVENDER HONEY. WE THANKED HER + SHE TOLD ME TO SET SOME OUT FOR THE PIXIES. I WOULD.

chamomile

lila's garden
NECKLACE

Silver flower specimens of metal clay pressed from carved molds and gleaming stone drops create a necklace of delicate beauty. These can be used as links or pendants, so make extras for earrings and bracelets. Try setting stones into the surface for extra sparkle, especially for earrings.

PRESSED-FLOWER PENDANTS

1~ Press 6 balls of metal clay into polymer clay stamps (see page 41 for instructions and be sure to lightly coat stamps with olive oil). Start in the center and continue toward the edge. Carefully peel away from the stamp. *Note: this project was created with 1¼" (3.2 cm) pressed-flower pendants.*

2~ With a needle tool or toothpick, poke holes at the top and bottom of the metal clay pressings. They don't have to be perfect—a craft blade can be used to clean up the holes when they are dry.

3~ Fire when completely dry and polish. Use flat-nose pliers to gently straighten the pieces if they come out of the kiln misshapen.

PRESSED-FLOWER PENDANT MATERIALS

Metal clay

Olive oil

TOOLS

Metal clay toolbox (page 25)

Polymer clay stamps

Needle tool or toothpick

Craft blade

Flat-nosed pliers

NECKLACE MATERIALS

16 labradorite 6mm faceted coins

6 silver metal clay 20×13mm flower pendants

10 pink 5×10mm chalcedony drops

20 labradorite 3×7mm drops

4 white 6×9mm chalcedony drops

6 labradorite 7×11mm drops

18" (40.6 cm) of silver 2×5mm cable chain

100" (2.54 m) of silver 26-gauge wire

2" (5 cm) of silver 5mm rollo chain

TOOLS

Wire toolbox (page 16)

FINISHED SIZE

41½" (105 cm)

NECKLACE INSTRUCTIONS

1— Attach a 1½" (3.8 cm) length of silver 2×5mm cable chain, using 1½" (3.8 cm) of silver 26-gauge wire. Create a simple loop, attaching to the end of the chain. String 1 labradorite 6mm coin and connect it with another simple loop to 1 silver 20×13mm metal clay link.

2— Make another wire-wrapped link using 1½" (3.8 cm) of wire to connect the metal clay link (from the previous step) to a 1½" (3.8 cm) length of 2×5mm cable chain, strung with 1 labradorite 6mm coin. Use 2" (5 cm) of wire to create a wire-wrapped dangle, attaching to the bottom loop of the labradorite coin link, strung with 1 pink 5×10mm chalcedony drop. Count down to the third-to-last link in the cable chain; use 1½" (3.8 cm) of wire to create a wire-wrapped dangle strung with 1 labradorite 3×7mm drop.

3— Use 1½" (3.8 cm) of wire to create a wire-wrapped link strung with 1 labradorite 6mm coin, attaching the length of chain from the previous step to 1 metal clay 20×13mm pressed link. Attach a 1½" (3.8 cm) length of silver 2×5mm cable chain to the pressed metal clay link, using 1½" (3.8 cm) of silver 26-gauge wire, strung with 1 labradorite 6mm coin. Use 2" (5 cm) of wire to create a wire-wrapped dangle, attaching to the bottom loop of the labradorite coin link, strung with 1 pink 5×10mm chalcedony drop. Count down three links in the cable chain; use 1½" (3.8 cm) of wire to create a wire-wrapped dangle strung with 1 labradorite 3×7mm drop. Count down another three links in the cable chain; use 1½" (3.8 cm) of wire to create a wire-wrapped dangle strung with 1 labradorite 3×7mm drop.

4 ~ Use another 1½" (3.8 cm) length of wire to create a wire-wrapped link strung with 1 labradorite 6mm coin, attaching the 2×5mm cable chain from the previous step to 1 metal clay 20×13mm pressed link. Attach a 1½" (3.8 cm) length of silver 2×5mm cable chain to the pressed metal clay link, using 1½" (3.8 cm) of silver 26-gauge wire, strung with 1 labradorite 6mm coin. Make another wire-wrapped link using 1½" (3.8 cm) of wire to connect the metal clay link to a 1½" (3.8 cm) length of 2×5 cable chain, strung with 1 labradorite 6mm coin. Use 2" (5 cm) of wire to create a fancy-wrapped dangle, attaching to the bottom loop of the labradorite coin link, strung with 1 pink 5×10mm chalcedony drop. Count down three links in the cable chain; use 1½" (3.8 cm) of wire to create a wire-wrapped dangle strung with 1 labradorite 3×7mm drop. Repeat three times, adding 3 more wire-wrapped labradorite dangles (for a total of 4).

5 ~ Repeat Steps 1 through 4 for the second half of the necklace. Connect the top of the necklace with 2 wire-wrapped links, attaching 3" (7.6 cm) of silver 2×5mm cable chain between the two tops of the halves of the necklace, using two 1½" (3.8 cm) lengths of wire, each strung with 1 labradorite 6mm faceted coin.

6 ~ Connect the bottom of the necklace with 2 wire-wrapped links, attaching 2" (5 cm) of silver 5mm rollo chain between the two bottoms, using two 1½" (3.8 cm) lengths of wire, each strung with 1 labradorite 6mm faceted coin.

7 ~ Embellish the 2" (5 cm) of rollo chain with fancy-wrapped dangles. Use 2" (5 cm) of

wire to create a wire-wrapped dangle, attaching to the bottom loop of the labradorite coin link, strung with 1 pink 5×10mm chalcedony drop. For the same loop, use 1½" (3.8 cm) of wire to create a wire-wrapped dangle strung with 1 labradorite 3×7mm drop. For the first link of chain, use 1½" (3.8 cm) of wire to create a wire-wrapped dangle strung with 1 labradorite 3×7mm drop. For the next link, use 2" (5 cm) of wire to create a wire-wrapped dangle, strung with 1 pink 5×10mm chalcedony drop. The third link will have 2 dangles; use 2" (5 cm) of wire to create a wire-wrapped dangle, strung with 1 white 6×9mm chalcedony drop, and use 2" (5 cm) of wire to create a wire-wrapped dangle, strung with 1 labradorite 7×11mm drop. The next link will have only 1 drop; use 1½" (3.8 cm) of wire to create a wire-wrapped dangle strung with 1 labradorite 3×7mm drop. For the next link, use 2" (5 cm) of wire to create a wire-wrapped dangle, strung with 1 labradorite 7×11mm drop. The sixth link will only have 1 dangle; use 2" (5 cm) of wire to create a wire-wrapped dangle, strung with 1 white 6×9mm chalcedony drop. For the next link, use 2" (5 cm) of wire to create a wire-wrapped dangle, strung with 1 labradorite 7×11mm drop. Continue down the chain, using 1½" (3.8 cm) of wire to create a wire-wrapped dangle strung with 1 labradorite 3×7mm drop. Repeat this sequence in reverse for the remainder of the chain. End on the bottom loop of the labradorite coin link, using 2 dangles, strung with 1 pink 5×10 chalcedony drop and 1 labradorite 3×7mm drop.

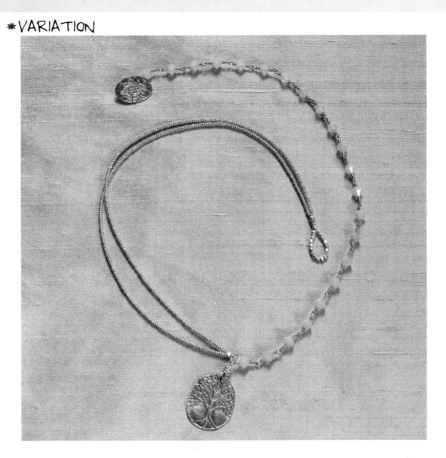

Make this simple necklace with a metal clay button, a seed-bead loop, and a handfull of crystals. A metal clay button is the perfect toggle clasp. This style of necklace looks great layered with longer pieces.

❋ VARIATION

These earrings are lightweight, easy to make, and fun to alter in countless variations. Try using jump rings to connect a series of metal clay charms or bits of chain to wire wrap stones and dangle from the charms.

117

tidepool
treasures

June 13

The doorway opened onto a tropical beach, with large boulders of LAVA spotting the sand. Just then, we found our subject, sitting in the sand near a high outcropping of rock. She looked up when we were a few yards away + inclined her head to us. She asked if we would like tea + pointed to the ROCKS nearby. I saw the opening in the wall, surrounded by palms and orchids. She dove into the water, a bright silver fish tail flashing in the sun + waved us to the opening.

We entered the cave and found ourselves in a large space; greenish light filtered down onto a small pool of water in the center. The MERMAID, CALLED MYOKO, popped up from the pool + smiled.

"See, I have a secret entrance! Usually, that door cannot be seen," she said, rising out of the pool.

My eyes adjusted to the dimness + I saw the walls + floor sparkled with PINK CRYSTALS + SEA GLASS piled in large clamshells. Myoko set a small table with a worn cast-iron tea service, including a little brazier to heat the water. I asked her how she came to live in such a MAGICAL place + a sadness drifted over her serene face.

"I once lived with many of my kind + life was carefree. All that changed the day my mother decided to go above to look at the shore. She loved land + the strange plants + animals. We swam close to some fishing boats + she was captured + killed. . . . I swam for days, stopping only when I couldn't swim any longer." She stopped + her eyes shone with unshed tears.

She took a deep breath, smiled + began serving the tea. It tasted like roasted rice. We sat in her sparkling haven, hearts heavy with her loss. I felt like walking + asked Tom if he wanted to come. We left the cave to face the BRILLIANT BLUE of the Pacific. He sat on a rock + played Hawaiian songs while I combed the shoreline. Myoko called out to me from under a rock bridge that ended in the water.

She sat on a SMOOTH ROCK with her SILVER TAIL submerged in a shallow TIDE POOL. The current moved fast, churning TINY WHIRLPOOLS before dragging back into the sea. What the water left shimmered + glowed in the sun + I picked up handfuls of SMOOTH PEBBLES OF SEA GLASS before the tide rushed back in. Thinking of what I was to create for her, I remembered seeing the shells filled with the gems, sharp at first, then TUMBLED IN THE SEA, which had smoothed the edges into something BEAUTIFUL.

tidepool treasures

Rings and pendants created from tumbled sea glass are forever captured in silver. This technique won't provide exact results every time because variations in glass, microscopic debris on the surface, and other pieces in the kiln can greatly affect the outcome. Plus, the metal may shrink and the glass may bulge out of its bezel. Sea glass has a tendency to change color: greens tend to stay the same, clear turns opaque, and browns get lighter. Find pieces of sea glass with no air bubbles that look smooth and clean.

NECKLACE MATERIALS

10 silver 2mm cornerless cubes

92 gradated watermelon tourmaline 5mm rondelles

90 silver 1½mm seed beads

1 embedded sea glass pendant

2 silver 2mm crimp tubes

18" (46 cm) of bronze .0014-gauge flexible beading wire

1 metal clay toggle (see page 29 for component instructions)

2 silver 6×2mm Thai spacers

TOOLS

Wire toolbox (page 16)

NECKLACE INSTRUCTIONS

1— String 1 silver 2mm crimp tube onto the wire and attach to half of the toggle. String 1 silver 6×2mm spacer and 3 silver 2mm cornerless cubes.

2— String 1 tourmaline 5mm rondelle and one 1½mm seed bead. Repeat forty-four times and string 1 tourmaline 5mm rondelle. Be sure to arrange the watermelon tourmaline in a gradated pattern, moving from black to crimson, highlighting greens and oranges in between. String 2 silver 2mm cornerless cubes.

3— String the sea glass pendant and follow Steps 1 and 2 in reverse to complete the other half of the necklace.

EMBEDDED SEA GLASS MATERIALS

Metal clay

Sea glass (varying sizes according to project)

Fine silver wire

Slip

Stones (optional)

TOOLS

Metal clay toolbox (page 25)

FINISHED SIZE

16" (41 cm)

EMBEDDED SEA GLASS IN SILVER

1— Roll out a sheet of metal clay. It can be quite thin because the sea glass will also give the finished pendant support. Place the glass in the center of the sheet, with a ½" (1.3 cm) border on all sides. Press the metal clay up and around the glass, smoothing it down and pushing out any air bubbles. Lock the piece in by enclosing the glass with a metal clay lip, so it won't pop out after firing. Smooth the metal clay and let it dry.

2— Either make a bail or use a jump ring made out of fine silver wire and attach it to the pendant with slip, making sure it grabs. Place on a hot plate to dry.

3— Decorate around the glass with set stones or balls of metal clay attached with slip, if desired (see pages 32–35 for stone-setting instructions).

4— Let the piece dry. Examine for cracks and patch with slip, if necessary. Check the surface of the glass for metal clay and remove, if present. Metal clay will fume the glass during firing. Fuming is when particles of metal attach in a thin coating to a surface. In this case, the silver particles in the metal clay will cloud the surface of the glass with a metallic sheen after firing. Use a wet paintbrush to remove any metal clay on the exposed glass.

5— If firing multiple pieces at once, make sure they are not touching and that they are right side up. If they are too close to one another, the glass will fume. This isn't necessarily a bad thing, because the haze can look interesting. The pieces tumble nicely. Remember that because the melting point of glass is far lower than that of metal clay, the glass will reach a viscous state and expand, creating a domed effect. If the pieces are not right side up, the glass will melt all over the bottom of the kiln. Keep in mind that some glass will turn different colors when exposed to high temperatures.

✳VARIATION

Instead of sea glass, substitute tektite. This olive-green tektite, a natural glass rock found only at the impact sites of meteorites, will retain its shape and color.

121

melusine's gift BRACELET

June 14

Tom rapped the bronze hand knocker several times, waiting for someone to open it.

"Maybe she's out back," he said, turning to the path along the house. The path ended in a high gate to the backyard + we entered through an arbor of CLEMATIS. The ocean was an uninterrupted stretch of dark blue, framed by SCARLET MAPLES. A splash came from the pool + a head of dark hair peeked at us from the edge.

"What are you doing here?" the woman yelled angrily.

"We have an appointment for the fourteenth. At two o'clock," Tom said, looking confused + slightly put out. We stood awkwardly to the side, unsure of what to do. She heaved a sigh + said with exasperation, "Fine, if Mirabelle sent you, nothing you see here will surprise you" + with that, she rose out of the pool, her top half a woman, her lower half a scaly green serpent tail. I held my breath, then let it out. Tom spoke for me, telling our names.

"I'm sorry for shouting. My name is MELUSINE," she said as she slithered upright in our direction. Watching the motion filled me with some primitive urge to flee. Instead, I said, "Are you the MELUSINE from the FRENCH fairy tale?"

Yes, I am. That story happened 761 years ago." "Is it true?" I asked.

"Most of it is. I was asked by a handsome king for my hand in marriage, with one condition, set by my kind, the fair folk: I was to have Saturdays all alone in a private house. He agreed he would not look upon me on that day, or I would be forced to leave forever. We lived happily for many years + we had many children. The day came when his conniving brother convinced him I was being untrue, so he stole into my house + witnessed my secret. I kissed my children + fled the kingdom."

"So you lost everything!" I exclaimed, shocked by the tale.

"Yes, I believe I did suffer for my husband's faithless act." She stared out at the sea, + then said, "I'd like to show you something." We followed her into the house + I was surprised to see painted portraits covering every surface of the walls.

"Who are they?" Tom asked. The date on a portrait of a pretty girl in VELVET read 1548. Another was dated 1847, and all were PAINTED in a similar style.

"I painted my CHILDREN, my grandchildren . . . these are all my descendants," she said, her voice quiet + wistful.

I felt my throat close as I realized how hard it had been to stay away from her family + I thought my heart would burst.

"They're beautiful," I said.

melusine's gift
BRACELET

❧ Open-backed silver bezels embrace little paintings of butterflies and bits of poems, preserved forever under a drop of resin. This project can be created with a few different bezel techniques, including bezel wire and bezels made from clay. The ones pictured used fine silver bezel wire. Also, it can be worn as either a bracelet or a necklace. The open wire-wrapped loops on either end of the bracelet make it ideal for turning into a necklace with the simple addition of two lengths of ribbon fed through the loops. ❧

BUTTERFLY BEZEL MATERIALS

Bezel wire

Metal clay

Slip

Illustration

Gel medium

Resin

TOOLS

Metal clay toolbox (page 25)

Resin toolbox (page 45)

Ring mandrel

Texture stamp

Paintbrushes

Needle tool or toothpick

Craft knife

BUTTERFLY BEZELS

1— To create the 5 bezels, wrap bezel wire (or a thin strip of metal clay) around a ring mandrel to achieve the desired size (18×24mm). Press both sides to make an oval. Use a texture stamp (see page 41 for instructions) to press out an oval from metal clay slightly larger than the bezel—a little more than $1/8$" (3 mm). Press the bezel into the clay oval and remove the center piece.

2— Brush slip over the entire area, ensuring that there are no cracks and that the bezel fuses with the border. Use a needle tool or toothpick to poke a hole on both sides of the bezel in the pressed metal clay frame. Add small balls of metal clay around the bezel, attached with slip, for decoration.

3— Place the piece on a hot plate to dry. Check the holes and bore out with a craft knife to tidy the edges, if necessary. Also look for cracks around the bezel wire and repair with slip, if needed.

4— Fire and polish.

5— Use the finished bezel as a template to gauge how big to make your illustration. Trace and cut out with a craft knife. Trim the edges so that the illustration easily fits inside the bezel. Coat one side with gel medium and allow it to dry. When it is dry, repeat for the other side. This will protect the paper that your illustration is on from becoming permeated with resin.

6— Pour the resin (see pages 43–47 for full instructions on pouring resin and embedding inclusions, such as your illustration) and allow to set up completely.

BRACELET MATERIALS

5 silver 18×24mm butterfly bezel links

4 rose satin 4mm Swarovski crystal bicones

4 indicolite 4mm Swarovski crystal bicones

4 sapphire 4mm Swarovski crystal bicones

4 black diamond AB 4mm Swarovski crystal bicones

4 satin peach 4mm Swarovski crystal bicones

4 Indian pink 4mm Swarovski crystal bicones

30" (76 cm) of fine silver 24-gauge wire for homemade balled head pins (or 24 silver 1" [2.5 cm] balled head pins)

12" (30 cm) of sterling silver 24-gauge wire

1 silver 24x10mm S-clasp for a bracelet

TOOLS

Wire toolbox (page 16)

FINISHED SIZE

8½" (22 cm)

BRACELET INSTRUCTIONS

1— To make your own balled head pins, measure out and cut 24 lengths of 1¼" (3.2 cm) of fine silver 24-gauge wire. On a heatproof surface, use pliers to hold one end of the wire. Dip the other end into a butane torch flame. The tip of the wire should be at the very point of the inner blue flame. This is the hottest part of the flame. Hold the wire in the flame until the silver begins to melt and ball up. Adjust the wire, so that the ball does not fall off. When about ¼" (6 mm) has balled up, drop the balled wire into a quench bowl. Do not get your pliers wet because the box joint will rust. After a few seconds, retrieve your head pins from the quench pot (they should be completely cooled when they are immersed in the water). Dry the head pins off. Using two pliers, hold the head pin and do a half-twist of the ball. This work hardens the balled head pin and prevents the tip from popping off while working with it.

2— Using 2" (5 cm) of sterling silver 24-gauge wire, wire wrap the 2 silver 18×24mm bezel links together, forming the wrap a ½" (1.3 cm) long between the links. Repeat to connect the remaining 3 bezel links. Use two 2" (3.8 cm) lengths of sterling silver 24-gauge wire to create wire-wrapped links for the ends of the wire-wrapped bezel bracelet. Leave the loops open on each end.

3— To form dangles, using the 1" (2.5 cm) head pins, wire wrap 1 of each color crystal between the bezels on the ½" (1.3 cm) wire-wrapped link attaching the bezel links. Attach the S-clasp to each end.

BACK OF BRACELET BEZELS

DANGLES

These butterfly images can be copied to use inside your own bezels.

rainfall
NECKLACE

June 17

GETTING AROUND AMSTERDAM HAD ITS ISSUES, SUCK AS NOT GETTING RUN OVER BY THE BIKES THAT RUSHED BY. TOM LED ME THROUGH THE RIJKS-MUSEUM, SO I COULD SEE THE DUTCH MASTERPIECES. WE STOPPED BEFORE THE VERMEER PAINTING THE GIRL WITH A PEARL EARRING + HE SAID SOFTLY, "I THINK YOU'RE FAR MORE BEAUTIFUL," THEN CONTINUED ON TO THE NEXT PAINTING. I FELT MY FACE FLAME SCARLET.

WHEN THE TIME OF OUR APPOINTMENT CAME, WE HURRIED THROUGH THE EN-TRANCE OF THE BOTANICAL GARDEN, HOPING WE WEREN'T TOO LATE TO GET IN. WE FOUND OUR QUARRY IN THE DESERT SECTION, IN A SMALL DRAGON TREE POTTED IN A PLASTIC TUB. THE WOOD NYMPH THAT LIVED IN THIS LITTLE TREE WAS SMALL + DUSKY SKINNED, WITH WHITE-GOLD HAIR + THE DEEPEST BLUE EYES I'D EVER SEEN. SHE GOT UP + SMILED AT US, A TOUCH FORLORN. WE INTRODUCED OURSELVES + SHE TOLD US HER NAME, ADA.

"HOW DID YOU GET HERE, ADA?" I ASKED, WATCHING HER FIDGET WITH A TWIG.

"ONE DAY MEN CAME + DUG UP MY TREE! I'M TOO SMALL TO MAKE THEM GO AWAY, SO THEY POTTED MY TREE IN THAT POT." SHE POINTED AT THE PLASTIC, MAKING A FACE. "I MISS MY SISTERS + THE BIRDS . . . AND MY TREE IS NOT WELL. I THINK I WILL DIE, TOO."

SHE SPOKE WITH THE CONVICTION OF ONE SENTENCED TO DIE + HER SITUATION RANKLED MY SENSE OF RIGHT. I HAD AN IDEA + WHISPERED IT TO TOM. HE NODDED. WE FOUND A PLACE HIDDEN BY OVERGROWN TANGLES OF LEAVES + WAITED UNTIL EV-ERYONE LEFT. WE SNUCK BACK INTO THE DESERT ROOM + FOUND IT LOCKED. TOM SIGHED, THEN KICKED THE DOOR DOWN. WOW. WE RUSHED OVER TO ADA, + TOM SET UP THE TRAVEL BOX. I COULD HEAR FOOTSTEPS HURRYING IN OUR DIRECTION. A DOORWAY FLICKERED OPEN + WE DRAGGED THE HEAVY POT TOWARD THE DOOR. THE SECURITY GUARD WAS JUST OUTSIDE + YELLED SOMETHING IN DUTCH THAT I GUESSED WAS "STOP!" HE RAN TOWARD US. UNSURE AS HE REALIZED WHAT HE WAS SEEING, HE STOPPED AS WE FLUNG OURSELVES THROUGH, SHUTTING THE BOX BEHIND US.

WE WHOOPED + DANCED IN VICTORY, TOM LIFTING ME IN A BIG HUG. SHE BEGAN TO CRY + LAUGH, AS SHE SPOTTED A NYMPH BOUNDING TOWARD HER. WE WATCHED AS SHE WAS JOINED BY MORE + MORE RELATIVES, ALL REJOICING IN THEIR GOOD FORTUNE. BEFORE WE LEFT, I ASKED ADA WHAT SHE WANTED ME TO MAKE FOR HER + SHE REPLIED, "SOMETHING THAT REMINDS ME OF RAIN + THE NIGHT SKY. I NEVER THOUGHT I'D FEEL RAIN ON MY FACE EVER AGAIN."

"THANK YOU."

rainfall NECKLACE

A scattering of labradorite drops and faceted gems provide the backdrop to the deep blue pendant of polymer clay, resin, and silver. The pendant is a collection of techniques, sculptural scrimshaw, metal clay decoration, and buffed resin over a miniature sky painting. The bezel can also house other minute objects or photographs under the hazy surface. This is a beautiful way to add decoration to an otherwise simple pendant.

sky painting

To paint the sky within the bezel, use acrylic paint and a size 2 paintbrush. First, start with two small dabs of white and cerulean blue and mix thoroughly to get your background color. Next, apply the color by scumbling the paint into the bezel, to coat the interior. Then, while the paint is still wet, apply white dabs for clouds, slightly blending into the background along the bottom of the cloud. Touch up the clouds after the paint has dried using white paint.

RAINFALL PENDANT

BACK

1~ Make a bail to set into the clay. Make a small ring from metal clay. Allow it to dry. Press a small disc from the metal clay. Allow this to dry. Roll out a small ¼" (6 mm) log of metal clay, cut it in half, and attach it to the clay disc. Flare away from each other. These will prevent the bail from coming loose from the polymer clay pendant. Allow it to dry.

2~ Trim the metal clay ring with a craft knife to create a flat spot that will allow it to sit flush against the disc. Use slip to attach the ring to the disc. Allow the pieces to dry. Make the center by texturing a sheet of metal clay and cutting out a square. Then, use a round cutter to remove the middle from the square. Use a template from polymer clay to cut out 4 marquis shapes from a thin sheet of metal clay. Allow these to dry before attaching them to the square with slip. Add small balls of metal clay to decorate the edges. Fire and polish.

3~ Condition the polymer clay and form it into a thick disc, about 1½" (3.8 cm) across. Press the polished pieces in place—the bail at the top, the decorative face in the center—and use a wooden tool to scoop out the clay from the middle, forming a small, deep bezel. Gently press the polymer pendant onto a tile. Using a wooden tool with a square tip, push the tool into the surface, at least 1 mm deep, to create a design. Dry with a heat gun, then flip the pendant and make a design on the other side, which should still be soft. Bake.

4~ Use a wooden tool to pop off the decorative metal clay centerpiece on the inside of the centerpiece. This way if the tool leaves a mark, it's inconspicuous. Then fill in the scraped-away design on the polymer clay pendant with another color of polymer clay. Blend the fresh (uncured) polymer clay into the baked pendant, scraping away the excess. Bake again.

5~ Sand with graduating grits of sandpaper (400 to 2000) to reveal and polish the design. Attach the finished metal clay centerpiece to the pendant with a two-part epoxy adhesive. Paint the inside of the bezel with acrylic paints, and once dry, fill with resin. Be careful not to overfill!

RAINFALL PENDANT MATERIALS

Metal clay

Slip

Polymer clay

Two-part epoxy adhesive

Acrylic paint in white and blue

Resin

CLAY COLOR FORMULAS

Deep blue: 1 part teal, 1 part navy, 1 pinch foil

Deep brown: ¼ part bronze, ¼ part brown, 1 pinch foil

TOOLS

Metal clay toolbox (page 25)

Polymer clay toolbox (page 20)

Resin toolbox (page 45)

Texture tools

1

2

3

4

NECKLACE MATERIALS

17 labradorite 4mm faceted rondelles

2 labradorite 6mm faceted coins

24 labradorite 3mm rounds

2 labradorite 7mm faceted rondelles

78 sterling silver size 2mm cornerless cubes

1 labradorite 6mm round

1 crystal silver shade 8mm Swarovski crystal rondelle

1 labradorite 11x14mm bead

1 kyanite 10mm faceted coin

1 kyanite 19x9mm faceted simple-cut bead

23 cerulean 2mm seed beads

11 labradorite 7x4mm teardrops

4 light blue 6mm Swarovski faceted crystals

2 sky blue 10x9mm faceted cubic zirconia teardrops

4 indicolite 4mm Swarovski-encrusted rondelles

2 kyanite 20x13mm ovals

1 metal clay embellished polymer clay pendant

1 crystal silver shade 6mm Swarovski crystal rondelle

1 labradorite 8x14mm irregular oval

1 labradorite 10x8mm corrugated rondelle

1 clear 13x10mm faceted quartz chunk

1 smoky quartz 13x20mm simple-cut bead

23" (51 cm) of black 0.019 flexible beading wire

8 silver 2mm crimp tube beads

1 sterling silver 30mm toggle

2 sterling silver 2x5mm Thai daisy tubes

23 silver 4mm irregular Thai spacers

2½" (6.4 cm) of metal clay simple chain (see page 30 for instructions)

6' (183 cm) of silver 28-gauge wire

4 metal clay bead caps (see page 102 for instructions)

TOOLS

Wire toolbox (page 16)

FINISHED SIZE

19" (48 cm)

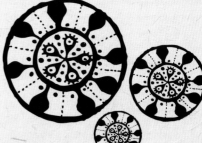

NECKLACE INSTRUCTIONS

1— Cut 8½" (22 cm) of beading wire. String 1 crimp tube and attach to half of the toggle. String 1 Thai tube, 1 irregular spacer, 10 labradorite faceted rondelles, 1 irregular spacer, 1 labradorite faceted coin, 1 irregular spacer, 5 labradorite 3mm rounds, 1 irregular spacer, 1 labradorite 7mm faceted rondelle, 1 irregular spacer, 6 cornerless cubes, 1 irregular spacer, 1 labradorite 6mm round, 1 irregular spacer, 1 crystal silver shade 8mm Swarovski crystal rondelle, 1 irregular spacer, 1 labradorite 11x14mm bead, 1 irregular spacer, 1 kyanite 10mm faceted coin, 1 irregular spacer, 1 kyanite 19x9mm simple-cut bead, 1 irregular spacer, and 1 crimp tube. String 19 seed beads, passing through the end of a 3-link handmade chain, back into the crimp tube, and through the irregular spacer and kyanite. Close the tube.

2— Using 1½" (4 cm) of silver 28-gauge wire, form a wire-wrapped dangle with 1 labradorite teardrop. Attach to the beaded loop. Using 1½" (4 cm) of 28-gauge wire, form a wrapped dangle with 1 labradorite teardrop. Attach to the first link. On the same link, use another 1½" (4 cm) length of 28-gauge wire to create a wire-wrapped dangle with 1 seed bead and 1 light blue 6mm Swarovski crystal. Using 1½" (4 cm) of wire, form a wire-wrapped dangle with 1 labradorite teardrop. Attach to the middle link. Repeat twice. Using 1½" (4 cm) of wire, form a wire-wrapped dangle with 1 labradorite teardrop. Attach to the last link. Using 1½" (4 cm) of wire, form a wire-wrapped dangle with 1 faceted CZ teardrop. Add to the last link.

3— Cut 3¼" (8.3 cm) of beading wire. String 1 indicolite Swarovski-encrusted rondelle, 1 crimp tube, and 16 cornerless cubes. Pass this through the last link of chain from the previous step and back through the crimp tube and rondelle, creating a beaded loop. Close the tube. String 1 metal clay cap, 1 kyanite oval, 1 metal clay cap, 1 indicolite Swarovski encrusted rondelle, 1 crimp tube, and 16 cornerless cube. Pass the end of the wire through the polymer clay pendant's bail and back through the crimp tube and the rondelle. Close the tube, forming a beaded loop.

4— Cut 8" (20 cm) of beading wire. String 1 crimp tube and attach to the remaining half of the toggle. String 1 Thai daisy tube, 1 irregular spacer, 3 labradorite 3mm rounds, 1 irregular spacer, 7 labradorite 4mm faceted rondelles,

1 irregular spacer, 1 faceted labradorite coin, 1 irregular spacer, 8 cornerless cubes, 1 irregular spacer, 1 labradorite 7mm faceted rondelle, 1 irregular spacer, 6 labradorite 3mm rounds, 1 irregular spacer, 1 crystal silver shade 6mm Swarovski rondelle, 1 irregular spacer, 1 labradorite 8×14mm irregular oval, 1 irregular spacer, 1 labradorite 10×8mm corrugated rondelle, 1 irregular spacer, 1 clear 13×10mm faceted quartz chunk, 1 irregular spacer, 1 kyanite oval, 1 irregular spacer, 1 crimp tube, and 10 labradorite 3mm rounds. Pass the end through the end of a 3-link metal clay chain and then back through the crimp tube and spacer. Close the tube, forming a beaded loop.

5~ Use 1½" (4 cm) of silver 28-gauge wire to form a wire-wrapped dangle with 1 seed bead and 1 light blue 6mm Swarovski crystal. Attach to the beaded loop. Using 1½" (4 cm) of 28-gauge wire, form a wrapped dangle with 1 labradorite teardrop. Attach to the first link. On the same link, use 1½" (4 cm) of wire to create a wire-wrapped dangle with 1 seed bead and 1 light blue 6mm Swarovski crystal. Using 1½" (4 cm) of wire, form a wire-wrapped dangle with 1 labradorite teardrop. Attach to the middle link. Repeat twice. On the same middle link, use 1½" (4 cm) of wire to form a wire-wrapped dangle with 1 seed bead and 1 light blue 6mm Swarovski crystal. Using 1½" (4 cm) of wire, form a wire-wrapped dangle with 1 faceted CZ teardrop. Add to the last link. Using 1½" (4 cm) of wire, form a wire-wrapped dangle with 1 labradorite teardrop. Attach to the last link.

6~ Cut 3¼" (8.3 cm) of beading wire. String 1 indicolite Swarovski-encrusted rondelle, 1 crimp tube, and 16 cornerless cubes. Pass this through the last link of the chain from the previous step and back through the crimp tube and rondelle, forming a beaded loop. Close the tube. String 1 metal clay cap, 1 smoky quartz 13×20mm simple-cut bead, 1 metal clay cap, 1 indicolite Swarovski-encrusted rondelle, 1 crimp tube, and 16 cornerless cubes. Pass the end of the wire through the polymer clay pendant's bail and back through the crimp tube and the rondelle. Close the tube, forming a beaded loop.

magpie
PENDANT

June 21

THE TREE HOUSE LOOKED LIKE NOTHING I'D EVER SEEN, A HOUSE BUILT AROUND A GIGANTIC TREE, THE BARK SMOOTH + TOAST BROWN. I WONDERED IF IT HADN'T GROWN OUT OF THE TREE ITSELF, WITH ITS ORGANIC LINES, ROUND WINDOWS LIKE PORTHOLES + SHINGLES IN THE SHAPES OF THE LEAVES. TOM + I WALKED UP TO A SMALL DOOR HIDDEN AT THE BASE OF THE TRUNK + KNOCKED. IT FLEW OPEN + A SMALL, DARK-HAIRED WOMAN WELCOMED US IN, USHERING US UP THE STAIRS THAT SPIRALED UP THROUGH THE TRUNK, SMALL KNOTHOLE WINDOWS LIGHTING THE NARROW STEPS.

A LARGE BLACK + WHITE MAGPIE SWOOPED PAST US + I GLANCED BACK TO ASK THE WOMAN IF THE BIRD WAS A PET OR IF IT GOT IN ACCIDENTALLY. THE WOMAN WAS GONE. I TURNED BACK TO FACE THE LANDING + THE WOMAN WAS BUSTLING ABOUT, ARRANGING A TRAY WITH A TEA SERVICE. THE WOMAN WAS THE MAGPIE!

THE BLOND WOOD WALLS WERE COVERED IN SHELVES + CASES, AND THE FURNITURE WAS SIMPLE, CARVED FROM DARK WOOD. WITHIN THE CASES + SHELVES + UNDER GLASS DOMES, THOUSANDS OF SPECIMENS OF ROCKS, FOSSILS, PODS, FEATHERS + INSECTS WERE METICULOUSLY LABELED + CATALOGED. I FELT LIKE I WAS INSIDE A WONDER CABINET.

THE WOMAN, ELINORE, SERVED A WONDERFUL TEA, WITH STRAWBERRIES + CREAM IN LITTLE CUPS + VANILLA CAKES. WHEN WE FINISHED TEA, I BROUGHT OUT MY SKETCHBOOK TO DRAW + TAKE NOTES. SHE ASKED IF SHE COULD SEE IT, HER EYES GLITTERING WITH CURIOSITY AS SHE EXAMINED THE BITS OF EPHEMERA GATHERED ON OUR TRAVELS. WHEN SHE FOUND THE CLUSTER OF SPECKLED FEATHERS, SHE LET OUT A WHISTLE + SAID REVERENTLY, "ANGEL FEATHERS . . . YOU HAVE SO MANY . . ."

"YEAH, I GOT THOSE IN VENICE, FROM ONE I KNOW THERE . . ." I SAID, AFTER SEEING TOM'S AMUSED EXPRESSION. "WOULD YOU LIKE A FEW?"

I HANDED HER SOME + SHE MORPHED INTO A MAGPIE, CARRYING THE FEATHERS TO A GLASS BOX. SHE WAS AT THE TABLE AGAIN, HUMAN FORM, SHOWING US HER FAVORITE COLLECTION, A CASE THAT INCLUDED BEAUTIFULLY COLORED EGGS FROM A PIXIE, A FIRE BIRD, AN EMERALD DRAGON + TROPICAL BIRD GIRLS. THE REST OF THE AFTERNOON WAS SPENT LOOKING THROUGH HER COLLECTIONS. SHE GAVE ME A BAG OF STAR SAPPHIRE BEADS, AS A TOKEN OF OUR NEW FRIENDSHIP, BUT IT MIGHT HAVE BEEN THAT I'D COMPLETED ONE OF HER COLLECTIONS.

WHEN WE RETURNED TO MY HOME, TOM HESITATED AT MY DOOR, WANTING TO SAY SOMETHING. WE STOOD THERE A MOMENT, REGARDING EACH OTHER.

"YOU LOOK REALLY HUNGRY, TOM. HOW ABOUT I FIX YOU MY SPECIALTY? ROAST PORK WITH PEARS + ONIONS . . . + MY SIXTEEN-LAYER CHOCOLATE CAKE."

"YEAH, I AM FAMISHED! THAT SOUNDS REALLY GOOD!" HE SMILED + WALKED INTO THE KITCHEN, BOTH OF US HAPPY TO EXTEND OUR LAST EXPEDITION.

magpie PENDANT

A silver egg collects wishes and dreams and the occasional bit of wonder. This piece also features fused silver chain that has been hammered for a glittery effect. For each pendant, you will need cork clay to create the hollow form, which will burn away during firing. Do not use Styrofoam to create hollow forms—it will produce extremely toxic fumes when it burns away in the kiln and give you a migraine.

NECKLACE MATERIALS

1 sunstone 10×13mm faceted bead

1 magpie pendant

2 Herkimer diamond 9×5mm beads

1 garnet 8mm faceted bead

1 cherry 8×12mm quartz bead

12" (30 cm) of silver 22-gauge wire

2 metal clay links, 1 set with stones

12" (30 cm) of fine silver 20-gauge wire formed into a chain with ½" (1.3 cm) ovals

1 shibuichi 20×6mm key toggle

3" (7.6 cm) of fine silver 22-gauge wire formed into a chain with ¼" (6 mm) ovals

TOOLS

Wire toolbox (page 16)

FINISHED SIZE

19" (48 cm)

NECKLACE INSTRUCTIONS

1— Using 2" (5 cm) of silver 22-gauge wire, wire wrap the sunstone faceted bead to the bottom bail of the pendant.

2— Using 2" (5 cm) of silver 22-gauge wire, wire wrap 1 Herkimer diamond to 1 metal clay link. Use another 2" (5 cm) length of silver 22-gauge wire to create a wire-wrapped link, strung with 1 garnet faceted bead, attaching to the end of the 12" (30 cm) fine silver chain.

3— Use 1½" (3.8 cm) of silver 22-gauge wire to create a wire-wrapped link, strung with 1 Herkimer diamond, attaching the end of the fine silver chain to the key toggle bar.

4— On the right side of the top ring of the egg pendant, use 2" (5 cm) of silver 22-gauge wire to create a wire-wrapped link, strung with 1 cherry 8×12mm quartz bead and the last metal clay link, to form the other part of the toggle.

MAGPIE PENDANT

MAGPIE PENDANT MATERIALS

Cork clay

White glue or jeweler's wax

Fresh metal clay (1" [2.5 cm] ball)

Slip

2 fine silver jump rings

4 cubic zirconias

Tiny objects to fill egg

Watch crystal

TOOLS

Metal clay toolbox (page 25)

Round cutters

Craft knife

Sculpting tool (optional)

Vermiculite or casting powder

Pliers (tape the tips)

1~ Make a 1½" (3.8 cm) egg out of cork clay, smooth the surface, and allow it to dry thoroughly (about a day). This process can be expedited with the use of a dehydrator. Do not use a warming plate because it will cook the cork clay and cause it to become misshapen and cracked.

2~ Use a paintbrush to coat the surface of the egg with white glue or jeweler's wax to seal the surface and make the metal clay stick.

3~ Roll out a thin sheet of metal clay and wrap it around the cork to form a wide belt. Trim the excess and press it into the cork. Cut two circles of metal clay to fit over the top and bottom of the egg. Press the edges of the circles and the belt around the egg together, sealing it so that the entire surface of the egg is covered and smooth.

4~ Use a cutter slightly larger than your watch crystal to cut a window into the front of the egg. Make a window frame by using a larger cutter and the cutter used to make the window hole from a sheet of metal clay. The frame should be a little wider than 1/8" (3 mm). This will allow depth for the prongs to sit.

5~ With a craft knife, cut 4 long triangles from metal clay about ¼" (6 mm) long. Allow to dry. Press them into each

side of the frame so that they are evenly spaced. Apply slip around the base of each to seal the joint between the triangles of metal clay and the frame. Press out 2 small discs of metal clay and attach to the top and bottom of the egg. Into each disc, press a fine silver jump ring into the center, forming a bail. Allow to dry. Set 4 cubic zirconias in small balls of clay, allow to dry, and then attach around the frame with slip (for more detailed stone-setting techniques, see pages 32–35).

6~ Scrape a design into the dry clay with a sculpting tool or leave it plain. Fire in a pile of vermiculite or casting powder (called investment) and position the egg pendant so that if it slumps, it can easily be bent to shape with a mallet without hitting the prongs.

7~ Tumble and fill with objects. Set a watch crystal across the opening and carefully bend prongs over the crystal to keep it in place. Use pliers that have the tips wrapped in tape. This will not only prevent the tips from marring the surface, but will also provide traction so the prongs don't slip.

1

4

5

mirabelle's
LOCKET

June 24

i WORKED ALL WEEK ON THE PROJECTS, THROWING MYSELF INTO THEM UNTIL I COLLAPSED, AWASH IN EXHAUSTION. THE WORK DISTRACTED ME FROM THE INEVITABLE SADNESS THAT WOULD BEAR DOWN ON ME WHEN I NO LONGER HAD MY EXCURSIONS WITH TOM TO LOOK FORWARD TO. I PUSHED THE THOUGHT ASIDE + WRAPPED EVERYTHING. I EXAMINED **THE LOCKET** I MADE FOR MIRABELLE, A PIECE TO SHOW MY GRATITUDE FOR ALLOWING ME TO MEET SUCH WONDROUS BEINGS + EXPERIENCE SUCH MARVELS. I WANTED THE LOCKET TO **REPRESENT THE SECRET WORLD** THAT SHE INHABITED + THAT I'D NEVER FORGET. THOSE EXPERIENCES CHANGED ME FOREVER. I REMEMBERED HOW AFRAID I USED TO BE, HOW MEETING PEOPLE SCARED ME, HOW UTTERLY WITHIN MYSELF I KEPT. I SMILED AT MY TRANSFORMATION, I'D NEVER BE THE SHY GIRL IN THE CORNER AGAIN.

TOM WAS WEARING A TUX. HE WAS THE HANDSOMEST MAN I'D EVER LAID EYES ON.

"I GOT HERE EARLY + BROUGHT THIS." HE HELD UP A GARMENT BAG THAT WAS SLUNG OVER HIS SHOULDER. "I TOOK THE LIBERTY OF PICKING OUT A DRESS FOR YOU." HE LOOKED AT MY SHOCK-FILLED FACE.

"WHAT'S WITH THE TUX + THE DRESS?" I SAID, FEELING DAZED.

"FOR THE **MIDSUMMER NIGHT BALL,** MY DEAR. YOU'VE BEEN INVITED." HE BEGAN TO OPEN THE BAG + SAID, "YOU'D BETTER HURRY. YOU DO NOT WANT TO SHOW UP LATE." I GRABBED THE BAG + RAN.

MIRABELLE STOOD NEAR AN ORNATE TABLE, HER DRESS **DEEP BLUE + SHIMMERING,** COMPLEMENTING THE **WIDE GOLD WINGS** SPREAD AT HER BACK. WHEN WE APPROACHED, TOM BOWED DEEPLY + SAID, "MY QUEEN, WE BRING THE OFFERINGS." I SHOULD'VE EXPECTED THAT, FROM WHAT I'D SEEN EARLIER.

WHEN WE WALKED THROUGH HER BACK GARDEN, A DOORWAY APPEARED IN THE SIDE OF A LARGE HILL. **IT OPENED TO ANOTHER WORLD,** A PLACE OF CONSTANT TWILIGHT, OF FLOWERS THAT TINKLED MUSICALLY LIKE GLASS, WHERE THE TREES GREW TALLER THAN SKYSCRAPERS. FAIRIES OF EVERY IMAGINABLE APPEARANCE FLOATED TOWARD THE LARGEST TREE. AS WE REACHED THE TREE, AN OPENING ALLOWED US TO ENTER A BALLROOM LIT BY FAERIES IN PAPER LANTERNS. I RECOGNIZED THE DANCERS AS **MY NEW FRIENDS,** ALTHOUGH HERE THEY WERE DRESSED IN GOWNS GLITTERING LIKE IRIDESCENT BEETLE WINGS. MIRABELLE SPOKE + THE DANCERS GREW QUIET, LISTENING.

CONTINUED ON PAGE 141 . . .

mirabelle's
LOCKET

A dazzling keyhole locket containing another world is protected under resin and flanked by precious stone artisan beads. This locket also features a rolled metal clay hinge, an extremely useful technique that can be used for books or box tops. The locket can also hold a tiny book or an accordion-folded paper with photographs on it.

LOCKET MATERIALS

Fresh metal clay
(1½" [3.8 cm] ball)

1 scrap polymer clay
(2" [5 cm] ball)

Slurry

2" (5 cm) of 20-gauge
wire (any kind is fine)

Thick slip

4 synthetic ruby 4mm
cabochons

4 clear synthetic stone
3mm faceted rounds

Image or sculpture to
encapsulate

Resin

Paint (for interior of
the locket)

TOOLS

Metal clay toolbox
(page 25)

Resin toolbox (page 45)

Oval cutter

Texture stamp

Square cutter

Wire cutters

Locket template (trace onto
paper with a pencil)

LOCKET

1— To create the bezel, begin by rolling out a thin sheet of metal clay. Cut out an oval about 1⅝" (4.1 cm). Place on a hot plate to dry. Roll another sheet onto a texture stamp and cut a thin strip of metal clay 4¾" wide × ¼" high (12 cm × 6 mm). Wrap the metal clay strip around a form, such as a square cutter or even a block made from polymer clay, to support the metal clay strip upright as it dries. This will form the walls of the bezel.

2— Place the upright metal clay strip on the oval of metal clay and use a brush with water to make a slurry with which to attach the bezel in the center. Make 2 rings for bails and allow them to dry. Also roll out 18 small balls and 12 tapered rice shapes from metal clay to decorate the bezel edge. Dry on a hot plate. Roll out a thin sheet of metal clay and wrap it around the piece of 20-gauge wire. Trim the excess to make a tube. Set on a hot plate. Trim the rings to fit the top and bottom of the oval and use slip to attach them both. Using the dry rice and ball shapes, make a pattern on the oval, wetting it down with a brush first.

3~ To make the hinge, cut the dry tube of metal clay into 3 pieces, attaching 2 along the top edge of the bezel with a thick slip. Reserve the third piece of tube for the top of the locket.

4~ To make the top of the locket, trace the form used to make the bezel onto paper, only make it slightly larger. Trace around the template onto a thin sheet of metal clay. Set aside and cut a small square from a textured sheet of metal clay. Lay the square on the front of the top locket piece, centering it and using slip to secure it. Cut a keyhole with a craft knife through the middle. Set on a hot plate to dry.

5~ Next, set 4 cabochons around the edge of the keyhole (see pages 32–35 for stone-setting instructions). Set 4 small stones at each corner. Then, dab slip between each stone and place a dry clay ball for decoration. Allow to dry.

6~ Brush thick slip onto the top middle edge of the locket face and push the clay tube into place. Make sure it lines up with the tubes on the bezel. Let it dry in place, then check the fit by sliding a wire through; adjust it so it opens easily and smoothly. Take the time to perfect it—making repairs during this stage is far easier than after the piece has been fired.

7~ Fire. Stick wire through the tubes on the bezel and tuck the ends. Fix any cracks or imperfections with slip. Once dry, polish. Encapsulate an image or sculpture in the bezel, filling it with resin.

1

2

6

NECKLACE MATERIALS

1 labradorite 14×7mm drop

1 metal clay and resin locket

3 Siam 4mm Swarovski crystal-encrusted rondelles

18 labradorite 4mm round beads

2 silver 18×13mm key barrel beads

8 indicolite 4mm Swarovski crystal bicones

8 black diamond 4mm Swarovski crystal bicones

4 sapphire 4mm Swarovski crystal bicones

2 green 8×15mm faceted quartz beads

2 green 10×21mm faceted quartz beads

10' (305 cm) of silver 22-gauge wire

1 silver metal clay 5mm toggle clasp (see page 29 for instructions)

20 silver 1½" (3.8 cm) balled head pins

TOOLS

Wire toolbox (page 16)

FINISHED SIZE

17" (43 cm)

NECKLACE INSTRUCTIONS

1— Wire wrap the 14×7mm labradorite drop to the bottom ring on the locket using 4" (10 cm) of silver 22-gauge wire and 1 siam 4mm rondelle. Set aside.

2— Use 2" (5 cm) of silver 22-gauge wire to create a wire-wrapped link, strung with 1 labradorite 4mm round, attached to half of the toggle. Use another 2" (5 cm) length of wire to make another wire-wrapped link, attaching it to the loop in the previous link to create a wire-wrapped link chain. Repeat seven times.

3— Make another wrapped link, stringing 1 silver 18×13mm key bead onto 6" (15.2 cm) of wire, attaching to the last link in the previous step. Create a wire-wrapped dangle tassel, added to the bottom loop of the key-bead link. Use 1½" (3.8 cm) head pins to make wire-wrapped dangles. Create a total of 5, using 2 indicolite 4mm bicones, 2 black diamond 4mm bicones, and 1 sapphire 4mm bicone.

4— Using 6" (15 cm) of silver 22-gauge wire, create a wire-wrapped link, strung with 1 green 8×15mm faceted quartz bead attached to the key-bead link. Use 4" (10 cm) of silver 22-gauge wire to create another wire-wrapped link, strung with 1 siam 4mm rondelle. Create another wire-wrapped dangle tassel, attaching to the bottom loop of the rondelle link. Use 1½" (3.8 cm) head pins to create 5 wire-wrapped dangles, using 2 indicolite 4mm bicones, 2 black diamond 4mm bicones, and 1 sapphire 4mm bicone.

5— Using 6" (15 cm) of silver 22-gauge wire, create a wire-wrapped link, strung with 1 green 10×21mm faceted quartz, attaching to the previous link and to the top ring on the locket.

6— Repeat Steps 2 through 5 for the other side.

CONTINUED FROM PAGE 137 . . .

"I SENT OUR WONDERFUL ARTIST TO VISIT YOU + TO CREATE A PIECE THAT CAPTURED SOMETHING OF YOUR PERSONALITY. I THINK SHE SUCCEEDED! **THERE IS MAGIC IN CREATION, RADIATING INTENT.** THEY RESONATE WITH HOPES + WISHES + BLESSINGS. AS THANKS FOR THE MAGIC SHE HAS BESTOWED UPON US, I GIVE HER GOOD FORTUNE FOR HER + HER LINE." A ROAR OF APPLAUSE RANG THROUGHOUT THE BALLROOM, FORCING TEARS TO PRICK MY EYES. I GAZED BLEARILY AT THE SMILING FACES OF FRIENDS, NOT REALIZING I LOCKED HANDS WITH TOM WHEN I BOWED + PRESENTED MY LAST GIFT TO MIRABELLE.

WE SPENT THE NEXT FEW HOURS WHIRLING AROUND THE DANCE FLOOR + TALKING WITH FRIENDS.

"MIRABELLE'S **PLAN WORKED,** THANKS TO YOU," SAID TOM, AS WE GLIDED ACROSS THE FLOOR.

"PLAN?" I ASKED, SMILING + WAVING TO MYOKO, WHO WAS SPLASHING IN AN ELABORATE BOWL ON WHEELS, DESIGNED TO KEEP HER WET.

"ALL THIS," HE WAVED HIS HAND OUT TO THE DANCERS, "WAS TO KEEP THEM FROM LEAVING THE HUMAN WORLD, TO REMIND THEM OF LIFE BEFORE, WHEN **THEY BROUGHT MAGIC TO EVERYONE THEY ENCOUNTERED.**

THE ONES WE WENT TO WERE ON THE BRINK OF LETTING GO OF YOUR WORLD. THEY ARE CAPABLE OF SO MUCH GOOD, BUT FOR WHATEVER REASON, THEY HAVE CHOSEN TO STAND IDLE."

"SO YOU'RE SAYING THESE FOLKS WANTED TO LEAVE MY WORLD FOREVER + STAY HERE?" THE THOUGHT SADDENED ME IMMENSELY.

"I THINK TALKING WITH YOU, INTERACTING WITH A HUMAN, REMINDED THEM OF THE PAST. OF **THE GOOD IN THE WORLD.**" I BALKED. I WAS THE SPOKESPERSON FOR GOOD?

THE THOUGHT LEFT ME FEELING HAPPY, BUT IT WASN'T ENOUGH TO QUELL THE SADNESS THAT OUR ADVENTURES WERE OVER. WE LEFT THE KINGDOM OF THE FAIR FOLK + TOM GRABBED MY HAND + WALTZED ME AROUND THE GARDEN AS DAWN BROKE.

"TOM, WILL YOU COME + VISIT ME, EVEN THOUGH OUR JOB IS DONE?" HE STARED AT ME, AS IF I HAD SPROUTED A HORN.

"I WOULD NEVER LEAVE YOUR SIDE, IF YOU ALLOWED ME TO BE WITH YOU." THEN HE KISSED ME + I REALIZED WHAT I KNEW ALL ALONG - THAT **MY HEART WAS ALREADY HIS.**

The painting inside the locket was created with gouche and watercolors. The technique is simple, start with a layer of water-color, then overlay with gouche. Creating the miniature paintings requires time and patience, but for the detail-oriented, it can be quite meditative. If you would like to include your own tiny paintings inside your jewelry, you can also paint on a larger scale and then scan and reduce it to fit inside your piece.

October 29

MIRABELLE'S GIFT OF GOOD FOR-TUNE DIDN'T OCCUR TO ME UNTIL I REALIZED **JUST HOW FORTUNATE** I'D BECOME. I DISCOV-ERED THAT THE PEBBLES THAT TUALA, THE SELKIE, GAVE ME WERE PRECIOUS- SAPPHIRES, TWO RUBIES + A VERY SIZABLE DIAMOND. THAT MEANT I DIDN'T HAVE TO FIND WORK. I COULD **COOK + MAKE ART TO MY HEART'S CONTENT.**

I MAINTAINED FRIENDSHIPS WITH MANY OF THE FOLKS THAT I MET. ANTONIA BECAME ACTIVE IN THE ARTS AGAIN, POSING WHEN SHE COULD OR WHISPER-ING TO POETS, ALLOWING THEM TO SEE HER AS A BEAUTIFUL WOMAN, AND **ONLY IN DREAMS WITNESS-ING HER TRUE FORM.** I HEARD THAT LAYLA OPENED A RESTAURANT AND + THAT IT WAS ONE OF THE BUSI-EST IN THE ENTIRE REGION, KNOWN FOR HER EXCELLENT CUISINE. LUELLE RENOVATED HER APARTMENT BUILDING + RENTED IT TO ARTISTS, MUSICIANS, + ONE OTHER GARDENER, WHO SEEMED TO HAVE TAKEN A SHINE TO HER. HER FAMILY DISCOVERED HER, AFTER AN ANONYMOUS TIP + VISITS REGULARLY.

TUALA SEEMS CONTENT - SHE ISN'T AS FEARFUL + GOES INTO TOWN ONCE IN A WHILE (AFTER HIDING HER SKIN IN A VERY SECRET PLACE). THESE DAYS, MYOKO SPENDS HER TIME RESCUING SURFERS FROM SHARKS + FOOLHARDY

SNORKELERS FROM DROWNING. THEY CHALK UP THEIR BRUSH WITH DEATH TO OXYGEN DEPRIVATION OR THE SUN BLINDING THEM. I HEARD FROM A RELIABLE SOURCE THAT SOME OF HER PEOPLE HAVE COME TO THE ISLANDS, TO TRY SAFER WATERS.

MELUSINE DECIDED THAT THE CENTU-RIES-OLD CURSE THAT KEPT HER FROM HER FAMILY HAD RUN ITS COURSE, + **SHE WOULD NO LONGER SUFFER IT.** SHE LOOKED AFTER HER DESCENDANTS' CHILDREN, WHICH WERE MANY, AFTER SHOWING THEM A GENTLY ALTERED FAMILY TREE THAT PROVED HER RELATIONSHIP. ELINORE SHARED HER COLLECTIONS WITH SCHOLARS + ART-ISTS, BY APPOINTMENT ONLY. I GUESS THAT **GOOD FORTUNE TOUCHED EVERYONE** THAT NIGHT AT THE BALL.

I FOUND ANOTHER TREASURE IN MIRABELLE'S GIFT. SHE RELEASED TOM FROM HER SERVICE, GRANTING BOTH OF US PERMISSION TO ENTER HER KINGDOM + GAVE US THE MAGICAL TRAVEL BOX, SO IT WOULD BE EASY TO VISIT OUR NEW FRIENDS + HER. OUR DAYS ARE SPENT TOGETHER, TRAVELING AROUND THE WORLD, TALKING WITH FRIENDS, PICNICKING IN BEAUTIFUL PLACES, ENJOYING DELICIOUS FOODS + **EXPLORING HIDDEN REALMS.** MOSTLY, TOM SINGS WHILE I DRAW + LISTEN, SKETCHING THE WONDROUS PICTURES IN THE MUSIC OF HIS VOICE.

inspiration
GALLERY

We all have a source of magic. For example, I find magic in botanicals. But magic is not only found in the exquisiteness of nature. It exists all around us. If you look for it. This part of the book features additional interpretations on the theme of *Enchanted Adornments*.

The fourteen artists featured here are forerunners in the field of mixed-media jewelry, and their styles range from classic to elegant and quirky to whimsical. The materials they use are both common and uncommon, but the way they have been combined and interpreted can only be described as curiously artisan.

When creating their pieces, many artists were moved by the sea. Others sought inspiration from fairy tales and folklore, flora and fauna, biology, the jungle, a forgotten garden, and the wondrous energy patterns inside us and surrounding us. Take a moment to feel gratitude for all of the magic that surrounds you and think about how you can invite more of it into your life. With this information, you will create your own magical mixed-media jewelry.

RETAINING THE SWELL
necklace

{JANE WYNN}

Jane used soldering and wirework to capture the feeling of reliquaries, the ocean, and beachcombing on lazy early mornings in September after a storm.

FINISHED SIZE 20" (51 cm)
MEDIA Brass, copper, Plexiglas, brass wire, seashells, salvaged estate jewelry, starfish, pearls, chandelier crystals, beads

FLYING HOME
necklace

{KATE MCKINNON}

Kate loved the look of the soft blue silk ribbon to complement the boa feathers at the tips. Techniques for making the fine silver metal clay chain can be found in Kate's own book, *Structural Metal Clay*.

FINISHED SIZE 7" (18 cm)
MEDIA Sterling silver tubing, fine silver wire, sterling silver chain, fine silver metal clay, feathers from a blue boa, silk ribbon, brass findings, fine pewter charms

145

SEA WAVES lariat

{LAURA ANN BELKIN}

Laura used wire wrapping and the polymer nail-studded technique to capture the mystery of the sea and the movement of the waves.

FINISHED SIZE 26" (66 cm)
MEDIA Faceted pearls, plated pewter bead caps, gold-filled chain, gold-filled wire, brass nail heads, gold-leaf foil, polymer clay

MAHALO, PENNY M necklace

{CANDICE WAKUMOTO}

Inspired by the dramatic beauty of the scenery of her island home and traditional folklore, Candice created this piece using advanced metal clay techniques and basic stringing techniques.

FINISHED SIZE 18" (46 cm)
MEDIA Metal clay, 22K gold, synthetic rubies, image transfer, black Tahitian pearl, sterling, rhodalite, garnet, vermeil, ametrine, and heishi pearls

QUEEN MAB'S FAERY PARADE
necklace

{MELANIE BROOKS}

Using basic plier work, stringing, knotting, and wire wrapping, Melanie made this piece as a costume accessory for a faery-themed convention she attended. While making it, she dreamed of an autumnal faery procession led by Queen Mab.

FINISHED SIZE 22½" (57 cm)
MEDIA Porcelain components, brass findings, glass leaves, pearls, amber, wire

VICTORIAN GARDEN necklace

{JEAN YATES}

In her yard as a child, Jean had an abandoned garden. She enjoyed imagining the ladies who used to sit and have iced tea there after playing games on the lawn. Using wire wrapping, she created a necklace that reminds her of her childhood, her family, and that garden.

FINISHED SIZE 15" (38 cm)
MEDIA Pearls, crystals, chain, polymer, metal clay, porcelain

OCEAN ABYSS
necklace and bracelet

{LORELEI EURTO}

Creating the piece around the components that mimic the flowing plant life that grows in watery depths of the ocean, Lorelei used simple stringing techniques. She was inspired by the magic that resides in these hidden fathoms.

FINISHED SIZES Necklace: 41" (104 cm); Bracelet: 8" (20 cm)

MEDIA Polymer clay beads, pewter links, lampwork glass, and various beads and findings

MERMAID'S BOUNTY necklace

{MARGOT POTTER}

The ancient tales of mermaids inspired this mélange of color and sparkle. Imagined as a trove of treasures gathered from the bottom of the sea, Margot used wire wrapping and stringing techniques to fashion this assortment of sea-inspired components into a talismanic necklace.

FINISHED SIZE 17½" (44.5 cm)

MEDIA Bronze coins, Netsuke mermaid, Swarovski elements, gold-plated Thai hill tribe drops, glass vial, glitter, wire mesh, poly chain and finding, gold-plated hammered chain, antique Chinese coin

KYANOS necklace
{CARTER SEIBELS}

This piece was inspired by the dynamic of objects and beings in the world. Carter was intrigued by the relationship of energy transferred by humans to the objects that they make and the energy humans absorb from the world. Using lampwork, stringing, wire wrapping, and resin techniques, she created this piece as a talisman, to attract positive energy to its wearer and her creations.

FINISHED SIZE 22" (56 cm)
MEDIA Silver clasp, seed beads, wire, handmade lampworked glass beads, fine pewter beads, nailhead

PODLETS lariat
{GAIL CROSMAN MOORE}

Using seed-bead weaving, wet felting, borosilicate lampworking, and felt embellishing (with Swarovski and vintage sequins and Japanese seed beads), Gail created this jewelry inspired by botany and biology.

FINISHED SIZE 31½" (80 cm)
MEDIA Beads, wire, lampworked beads, borosilicate glass, wool, felt, Swarovski crystal sequins, Japanese seed beads, vintage sequins, wet felting

149

AWAKENING necklace

{BETH HEMMILA}

With this necklace, Beth wanted to explore the idea of awakening the psychic mind and instinctual knowing. Hand stamping metal clay, she created three life-affirming charms that symbolize the desire for wilderness (tree), freedom (horse), and creativity (rabbit). She incorporated the charms, gemstone, and findings with wire wrapping.

FINISHED SIZE 24" (61 cm)
MEDIA Gems (peridot, garnet, carnelian, and plum freshwater pearl), silver wire, chain, findings, metal clay charms

PLAYING AMONGST SEA FOAM

cuffs

{KELLY RUSSELL}

Constructing a metal lace armature and covering it with fabrics and antique lace, Kelly embellished this mermaid-theme cuff with molded metal clay, appliqué, and bead embroidery. She was inspired by sea foam and the surface of the water as well as the mysteries that lie beneath.

FINISHED SIZE 8½" (22 cm)
MEDIA Metal clay pendant, metal lace, silver Charlottes, pearls, crystals, antique lace, fibers

CABINET OF CURIOSITIES necklace

{MELISSA J. LEE}

Melissa found inspiration in Renaissance-era cabinets of curiosities when designing and assembling this piece. She created the box and other fine silver components from metal clay and completed the piece by simply stringing the amber and garnet beads.

FINISHED SIZE 19" (48 cm)
MEDIA Fine silver divided box, bone and snake and bone clasp, ceramic beastie bead, taxidermist eye, polished half ammonite, polished half geode, rough-cut garnet, amber beads, leather cord, amethyst cabochon, findings, epoxy

JUNGLE FEVER necklace

{JAMIE HOGSETT}

The animal print polymer beads and vivid green inks inspired Jamie to explore the primal magic of the jungle. She used shrink plastic, wire wrapping, jump rings, and stringing to create this exotic necklace.

FINISHED SIZE 17" (43 cm)
MEDIA Polymer beads, sterling silver flower connectors, sterling silver clasp, beading wire, jump rings, eye pins and other natural brass findings, shrink plastic

151

troubleshooting

Working with the materials in this book is a matter of trial and error. With a little practice, you will easily master the techniques. The following guide will help you during periods of experimentation.

polymer

This clay is very forgiving and easy to work with, but occasionally there are strange mishaps that occur. Here are the most common problems, the reasons, and how to either fix them right away or prevent the same problems in the future.

Surface Cracks After Baking

POSSIBLE REASON This can happen when a core of polymer (or some other material) leaches the moisture from the topmost layer of clay. This can also happen if the clay isn't conditioned properly before using.

REMEDY Prevent cracking by baking pieces that include cores within a week or less of applying the top layer and always conditioning clay until soft and pliable before each use. The cracks can be patched by packing clay into them or applying liquid polymer to them and then baking again.

Still Soft After Baking

POSSIBLE REASON Soft spots can occur if polymer clay pieces are cured in an oven with uneven heat or inaccurate temperatures.

REMEDY Use an oven thermometer to make sure the heat is at the right temperature and turn the piece a couple of times if the oven doesn't heat evenly.

Muddy Colors After Mixing

POSSIBLE REASON Grayish clay happens when either dirt from your hands or fiber from dark clothing, such as blue jeans, gets on the surface.

REMEDY Prevent this annoyance by using baby wipes to clean hands frequently and wearing light-colored clothes while working with clay. Muddy clay can be used as cores or if the piece will be painted.

Crumbly, Hardened Clay Right Out of the Package

POSSIBLE REASON This usually occurs with old clay or if the clay was left in the sun, which will slowly dry it out.

REMEDY Prevent this from happening by storing clay in an airtight box, out of the sun. To soften clay, use a coffee grinder to chop clay into bits (once you use a coffee grinder for clay, dedicate it to this purpose), then run through a pasta machine until softened. This could take a while; to speed things along, use a drop of liquid polymer to help rehydrate it.

metal clay

Although metal clay is easy and fun to use, sometimes things can go wrong. Here are the most common aggravations and how to fix or prevent them.

Strange Spots & Discoloring on the Surface After Firing

POSSIBLE REASON Aluminum foil or an aluminum pan was used to set wet clay on.

REMEDY The pieces can be polished, but will still have marks, so remember not to use aluminum foil or pans in your workstation. Glass, plastic, and ceramic are best.

Brittle Metal After the Clay Is Fired

POSSIBLE REASON Weak pieces occur when clay isn't fired long enough and at a high enough temperature for the metal to fully sinter.

REMEDY Always fire pieces starting in a cool kiln set for 1,650°F (899°C) for two hours. There are a few exceptions for very thin and small pieces or repairs, but anything that needs to be strong should be fired as stated above.

Cracks After the Piece Is Fired

POSSIBLE REASON This usually occurs when making hollow forms—thin sheets of clay stretched over cork can split in the kiln as it shrinks.

REMEDY To prevent cracking in future pieces, make sure the sheets are even, with no thin spots. To repair cracks, use clay to patch the area and fire again or fire with a butane torch (see page 28 for instructions).

Chalky Areas in Fired Pieces

POSSIBLE REASON This can happen if pieces are thrown into a hot kiln and are still moist or if they aren't fired hot enough or long enough.

REMEDY The chalky areas are where the clay didn't fully sinter, which means the piece is weak and will break. To prevent this, dry and fire pieces properly. Try firing the pieces again for the full time and at the correct temperature; this should eliminate the problem.

Air Pockets in Fired Pieces

POSSIBLE REASON The clay was folded with air trapped in the clay.

REMEDY The bubbles are permanent, but prevent this in the future by wedging clay in the palms of your hands in a sort of rolling motion, rather than flattening and folding the clay.

Dried Out Unfired Clay

POSSIBLE REASON The clay was improperly stored, causing moisture to be released.

REMEDY Depending on how dried out the clay is, you can rehydrate it by grinding the clay down and adding water (as described on page 152).

mold making

Molds are useful, but they require patience and time to perfect. Below are common problems and how to solve them.

Mold Is Still Tacky After It Has Set Overnight

POSSIBLE REASON The mold compound could be old, or it was improperly mixed. Sometimes the rubber can separate if stored on a cold cement floor, so always place cardboard under chemical containers.

REMEDY Let the mold set under a light for another day. If still tacky, try and remove the master for cleaning. To clean out the mold, dig out as much of the rubber as possible, then use denatured alcohol to break down the residue.

Mold Has Lots of Air Bubbles Near the Master

POSSIBLE REASON The rubber was whipped, rather than gently folded when mixed, causing air bubbles, or the rubber was poured in one big dollop over the master, also trapping air.

REMEDY The bubbly mold can be used, if you don't mind scraping off imperfections in the resin. To prevent bubbles in the future, mix the rubber carefully and pour the rubber slowly into one corner of the mold, allowing gravity to move rubber into crevices.

Mold Sticks to the Master When De-Molding

POSSIBLE REASON No mold release was used before pouring rubber, or the mold release wasn't compatible with the rubber.

REMEDY Starting from the pour hole, peel the rubber away using a wooden tool to scrape rubber from the master. To prevent molds from sticking, check labels to make sure the release is compatible with the rubber.

resin

This material is beautiful and simple to work with, but it requires great care and attention for finished pieces to come out perfectly. Remember to keep all work surfaces covered with paper (for easy cleanup) and materials ready at hand before you begin, to prevent racing around with resin setting up in cups.

Foamy Looking After Resin Has Set Up

POSSIBLE REASON Foam occurs when moisture or porous items come in contact with resin.

REMEDY The resin can't be fixed, so start over or remove from the bezel with a product called Attack! by placing it in a jar with a lid and adding enough product to cover the bezel.

Allow the bezel to sit overnight and repeat the process until all of the resin is removed. To prevent future foaming, make sure all items are dry and porous papers are coated with gel medium to seal the surface.

Still Tacky After Curing All Night

POSSIBLE REASON Due to humidity, the piece may need extra time to set up.

REMEDY Position the mold under a light for heat, which will help the resin set up.

Inks Lift Off Paper & Into Resin, Distorting Image

POSSIBLE REASON When encapsulating drawings, paintings, or small scrolls with writing, inks can lift off of the paper, if the resin reacts with the ink.

REMEDY The lifted ink cannot be reversed, so the resin must be removed. To prevent this, seal items with gel medium.

Embedded Items Sink to the Bottom of Bezel or Mold

POSSIBLE REASON It is common for heavy items to sink and also common for lightweight items to rise because density is a factor to consider when embedding objects.

REMEDY This is tricky—the object can be removed, and some of the resin poured out, leaving only a layer that you want the object to rest on, so it has a floating appearance. The downside to this fix is that the object might set up in a weird shape before you get a chance to place it back into the mold or bezel, so really consider density when trying to float an object.

Doesn't Set Up After Days of Curing

POSSIBLE REASON This means the resin was either very old or it was mixed wrong. Some resins are measured by weight, others by volume, so it's important to read the ratios before beginning.

REMEDY There is no way to save resin, so it must be removed with a wooden tool to scoop out the sticky mess, using denatured alcohol to clean the rest.

stones for firing

Stones are a natural element to use with metal clay, but not all can withstand the heat of the kiln. Follow the guidelines below to make sure your stones are compatible with the high kiln temperatures necessary for metal clay.

SYNTHETIC STONES

Synthetic stones are best for firing in place due to their uniformity and lack of inclusions. They are designed to cast in place with molten gold and silver, so the temperatures necessary for firing metal clay should not damage them. The most common synthetic stones to use are ruby, sapphire, cubic zirconia, alexandrite, and emerald. Any synthetic stone should work.

NATURAL STONES

Some natural stones can withstand the kiln, but due to inclusions (which may have trapped air and cause the stone to explode), it's best to test a stone first. Lay a fiber blanket (available at ceramic supply shops) over the stone so it traps any pieces that may stick in the kiln walls if it does explode. Do not use expensive or precious stones to test! Prong or bezel set them after firing so the stone isn't ruined. Some stones that have been fired in place are hematite, garnet, peridot, white moonstone, topaz, labradorite, and obsidian. **DO NOT FIRE:** opal, pearl, bone, wood, or shells.

resources

Stones & Pearls

BEAD TRUST LLC
650 University Ave.
Berkeley, CA 94710
p: (510) 540-5815
beadtrust.com

I love the variety of stones, crystals, and glass, all at great prices on this site.

TALISMAN ASSOCIATES
2001-A Veirs Mill Rd.
Rockville, MD 20851
p: (800) 229-7890
f: (301) 762-2421
talismanbeads.com

An amazing array of pearls as well as semiprecious and vintage beads you will find here.

Silver Clasps & Beads

GREEN GIRL STUDIOS
PO Box 19389
Asheville, NC 28815
p: (828) 298-2263
greengirlstudios.com

Find lovely pewter and silver beads as well as clasps at my shop!

SAKI SILVER
625 Eveningstar Ln.
Cincinnati, OH 45220
p: (513) 221-5480
sakisilver.com

Gorgeous clasps and pendants are available from friendly folks.

STAR'S CLASPS
139A Church St., NW
Vienna, VA 22180
p: (800) 207-2805
f: (703) 938-0541
starsclasps.com

Here you will find a delicate and lovely variety of clasps and findings.

NA BO ROW
(252) 634-3436
sales@naborow.com
naborow.com

My favorite place to get silver spacers and beads in every imaginable shape.

Crystals

FUSION BEADS
13024 Stone Ave. N.
Seattle, WA 98133
p: (888) 781-3559
fusionbeads.com

All-encompassing supersite and store, Fusion specializes in crystals and everything else bead related.

PUDGY BEADS
1150 E. Wardlow Rd.
Long Beach, CA 90807
p: (562) 427-0018
pudgybeads.com

This is a good source for vintage German glass.

BEADS AND ROCKS
335 Virginia Beach Blvd.
Virginia Beach, VA 23451
p: (757) 428-9824
beadsandrocks.com

These are purveyors of hard-to-find vintage crystals.

Precious Metal Clay

RIO GRANDE
p: (800) 545-6566
riogrande.com

A great source for all of your silversmith needs.

METAL CLAY SUPPLY
225 Cash St.
Jacksonville, TX 75766
p: (800) 388-2001
f: (888) 331-6953
metalclaysupply.com

A nice place to find useful tools and equipment.

Findings

ORNAMENTEA
509 N. West St.
Raleigh, NC 27603
p: (919) 834-6260
ornamentea.com/TheShop/

This is a wonderful supplier of unique goods; a mixed-media superstore.

LIMA BEADS
p: (888) 211-7919
team@limabeads.com
limabeads.com

This amazing supplier boasts a huge selection of beads and findings.

SOFT FLEX COMPANY
PO Box 80
Sonoma, CA 95476
p: (866) 925-3539
f: (707) 938-3097
softflexcompany.com

This is a manufacturer of strong, flexible beading wire and purveyor of findings, beads, and tools.

Seed Beads

JANE'S FIBER AND BEADS
5415 E. Andrew Johnson Hwy.
Afton, TN 37616
p: (888) 497-2665
f: (423) 638-5676
janesfiberandbeads.com

Every kind of seed bead can be found at this site.

gallery contributors

LAURA ANN BELKIN is a multi-media artist from the Washington, D.C., area. She is best known in the "bead universe" for co-owning Talisman Associates Inc., with her mother, Naomi Belkin. Her paintings and drawings have been shown in Maryland-area galleries as well as published in studio annuals and magazines. Please visit her website at lauraannbelkin.wordpress.com.

MELANIE BROOKS is a ceramic artist, specializing in porcelain beads and jewelry. She lives and works from her studio home in the Detroit, Michigan, area and sells her work under the name Earthenwood Studio. She enjoys making jewelry components inspired by science fiction, fantasy, pop culture, mythology, and art history. Her own articles, projects, and works made with her beads have appeared in many beading publications. Please visit her website at earthenwoodstudio.com.

GAIL CROSMAN MOORE is a teacher, mother, small business owner, and award-winning artist. She divides her time between creating and showing her work and encouraging others to create their own. Recognition of her abilities appears in print, both in trade publications and in books in several different fields. Her work can be viewed on her website at gailcrosmanmoore.com.

LORELEI EURTO works full time in an art museum in upstate New York and creates beaded jewelry as a form of art therapy. She enjoys concocting beautiful multimedia designs. Her designs have appeared in magazine publications such as *Stringing*, *BeadStyle*, and *Step by Step Beads*. You can see more of her work at her Etsy shop, Lorelei1141.etsy.com, and on her blog, Lorelei1141.blogspot.com.

BETH HEMMILA, owner of HINT in Portland, Oregon, creates jewelry that tells a universal story. She has a background in art history and a degree in sculpture and printmaking. Her passion for sensual textures and memories aid the creation of her narrative jewelry. Each piece incorporates hand-sculpted silver charms that draw on ancient symbols from the natural world. Please visit her blog at hintjewelry.blogspot.com to discover the inspiration and stories behind her work.

JAMIE HOGSETT is a jewelry designer and the education coordinator for Soft Flex Company. She is the author of *Stringing Style* (Interweave, 2005) and coauthor of the Create Jewelry series: *Pearls, Crystals, Stones, and Glass*. Contact Jamie through her blog, jamiehogsett.blogspot.com.

MELISSA J. LEE makes beads from fine silver and designs jewelry. She is an intellectual property lawyer by training and enjoys reading mystery and science fiction books, knitting, and spending time with her young son (not necessarily in that order). Please visit her blog at strandsofbeads.blogspot.com.

KATE MCKINNON is an author, a metalsmith, and a seed-bead enthusiast who lives in her hometown of Tucson, Arizona. She teaches, travels, and shows her work internationally. Her recent book on metal clay has been a runaway best seller, with its focus on safe handling, unusual structural techniques, and easy ways to make rings to size. You can find her online shop, photo galleries, and popular blog on her website at katemckinnon.com.

MARGOT POTTER is the author and designer of five published jewelry-making books, a member of the Beadalon design team, an ambassador for Create Your Style with CRYSTALLIZED Swarovski Elements, an on-air jewelry expert at QVC, and a Ranger Ink–certified instructor. Margot writes two blogs, creates award-winning humorous how-to videos, and appears often as a host and a guest on podcasts, television, and Web videos. Please visit her website at margotpotter.com.

KELLY RUSSELL is an artist who works in a variety of media to bring her ideas to life. She loves to experiment and incorporate different techniques into her work. Kelly shares her experience, teaching what she knows about metal clay and polymer clays. Kelly has had her worked widely published in books and magazines. Please visit her website at beadfuddled.com.

CARTER SEIBELS is a glass jewelry artist and bead lover based in Berkeley, California. Carter's love of color and fascination with all things sparkly and shiny has led her down a path full of creative endeavors. Her glasswork has appeared in galleries, exhibitions, and publications nationwide, and her jewelry designs are regularly published in beading magazines. Please visit her website and blog at divaliglassjewelry.com.

CANDICE WAKUMOTO uses silver clay with fabrication and gemstones to create one-of-a-kind art jewelry. Her pieces have also been featured in several books and publications. This award-winning artist is a lifelong resident of Hawaii, residing on the island of Oahu with her husband, Paul, and poi dog, Cassie.

JANE WYNN is a mixed-media artist whose work spans a broad spectrum of media. Her work is characterized by the curious juxtaposition of found objects, utilizing vintage imagery and distressed treatments. After receiving her masters in fine art from Towson University in Maryland, she now works full time in her studio and teaches workshops around the world. She is the author of *Altered Curiosities: Assemblage Techniques and Projects*. Please visit her website at wynnstudio.com.

JEAN YATES is the author of the jewelry design book *Links*. Presently she is writing a column for *Australian Beading* magazine and planning her next book. Proud mother of five sons and grandmother of two, Jean lives in New York with her husband, Jim. Please visit her website at prettykittydogmoonjewelry .blogspot.com.

ABOUT the AUTHOR

Cynthia Thornton grew up in Orlando, Florida. As a child, she spent most of her time creating fantasy worlds for her dolls. She remembers her first box of Sculpey and the army of faeries she created with it, foreshadowing the career she would pursue as an adult. Not all time was spent frolicking and making clay creatures, however. She was no stranger to hard work. To help out the family, every day after school she and her siblings mowed lawns and pulled weeds for their father's landscaping business in the hot Florida sun.

Cynthia graduated from high school and got a scholarship to Columbus College of Art and Design.

After college, Cynthia spent the next several years as a freelance artist, a haunted house mask maker, and a garden art sculptor, to fund her dream business, Green Girl Studios. This business consists of carving and casting her designs in fine pewter and silver and selling them at shows around the country. In 2002, she moved the operation to California, where she met up with Greg Ogden, college friend, musician, and artist. They relocated to Asheville, North Carolina, and got married in a garden, dressed as faeries, wings and all. Their daughter, Azalea, was born in 2004 and insists on "helping" the family business by sculpting her own designs. Green Girl Studios attends thirty-five shows a year and their work can be found in shops across the country and all over Europe and Japan.

GREEN GIRL STUDIOS

Green Girl Studios was founded by Cynthia Thornton in 1997, with a minute collection of beads and pendants cast in resin. The early designs were inspired by Japanese ojime (sculptural beads used as a toggle to close boxes worn on kimonos). Today, the beads are no longer cast in resin but in fine pewter, silver, and shibuichi; they are still handmade and of the best-quality materials. The company, which started with one artist, is now a family operation, run by her husband, Greg, a fellow artist, cartoonist, and everyday philosopher. Cynthia's brother Andrew assists at trade shows and is a Brooklyn-based jewelry maker, artist, and writer. The company depends on close friends to distribute and manufacture the jewelry components. Over the years, loyal customers have become a circle of friends that has grown to include people in Australia, Japan, Europe, and South America.

index

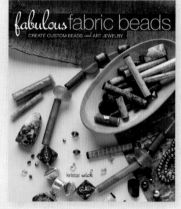
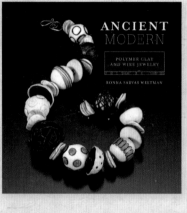